SELLING WITH MAGIC

How to Turn Your Presentations into Dollars!

MICHAEL JEFFREYS

Illustrated by Joyce Norton

Edited by Joy Wurdeman

Typeset by Judy Reese

Powerful Magic Publishing

Printed in the United States of America

First Edition

10 9 8 7 6 5 4 3 2 1

Library of Congress Catalog Card Number 89-092672

Jeffreys, Michael

Selling with Magic

1. Selling   2. Magic   3. How To's

ISBN 1-878407-00-7

DEDICATION

This book is dedicated to my mom, my dad, my sister Jill,
and to Uncle Jerry, who's always been there for me.

Also, I'd like to give a special thanks to Joyce Norton, my artist.
Her ability to take Harry, our "Fearless Wizard" and
make him come to life on paper is truly magical!

Michael and his ". . . aaah, wife, Morgan Fairchild, yeah that's it."

Michael discussing the lack of good quality scripts in Hollywood while sharing a cold one with Harry Anderson.

Michael "checking out" Joan Collins.

Michael getting a thumbs up from film critic Roger Ebert. (As an attractive fan points to her favorite magician.)

WARNING: FAILURE TO PROPERLY PRACTICE
THE TRICKS IN THIS BOOK MAY RESULT IN
EXTREME EMBARRASSMENT.

CONTENTS

CONTENTS (CONT)

INTRODUCTION

With today's competition in the sales and business world becoming increasingly competitive, any tool you can use to make yourself STAND OUT and BE REMEMBERED should be utilized to its fullest. MAGIC is a powerful tool that can turn a normal, ho-hum presentation into an impressive, dynamic, exciting sales pitch that leads to a signature on the bottom line.

Whether you sell a product or a service, whether you work for yourself or a company, the book you now hold in your hands can lead directly to increasing your personal income. By selecting and learning the tricks from this book that are right for your needs, you will be able to present your message in a new and exciting way — a way that most people have never seen before.

SALES PRESENTATIONS

For example, imagine you're giving a presentation to the department heads of a company whose account would mean tremendous income to your company, as well as to you personally, in the form of a large commission check. You know that if you go in with the same old dog and pony act, the decision makers, who've just about seen it all, probably won't bite.

So instead, you begin your presentation by taking out an obviously fake $100.00 bill, which you hold up for all to see. In a commanding voice you say, "Don't be fooled by cheap imitations!" You then proceed to tear up the fake $100.00 bill, stating, "While they may look genuine, there's a good chance they may not live up to their billing!" You then take the torn pieces of bill and make them into a little packet. Continuing, you say, "At XYZ industries, our products are guaranteed to be 100% genuine, to do all the things we say they'll do, or your money back." With that you open up the crumpled up pieces of bill and, much to the amazement of your mesmerized onlookers, you're now holding a brand new, genuine, $100.00 bill! (Trick #8).

Through the use of one simple magic trick, you have shown your clients that you are UNIQUE and CREATIVE. Because of this, they will sit up and take notice to what you have to say! That's what magic does — it grabs people's attention! It gets them excited! Why? Because they're seeing something they can't explain, something that defies logic.

COLD CALLING

Cold calling, something that all salespeople must do from time to time, becomes fun when combined with magic. Imagine walking up to the secretary or receptionist of an office and making a flower appear for her out of the air! (Trick #5). You've helped to make her day a little brighter. And the next time you call to talk to her boss — your call goes right through! You've used magic to build rapport with the office staff in a positive way, a way that makes them want to go out of their way for you.

ICE BREAKERS

Included in the book are many tricks which can be used as ice breakers at business functions; those situations where you want to make an IMPACT on an important client, but the situation isn't quite right for a formal meeting. Using magic, you now have a tool with which to make a positive, lasting impression.

Imagine you're attending a meeting of your local chamber of commerce, and the CEO of a large advertising firm is standing right next to you. You have been trying to do business with his company for the past year, but haven't been able to get your foot in the door. Now suppose you seize the moment to pull out a Bic ball-point pen and say, "Excuse me, Mr. Jones, have you seen these new disposable pens?" And then you make the pen disappear right before his eyes! (Trick # 2). Think of the impact that would have on him! At the very least, the door would be open for you to give him your business card and possibly set up a meeting.

Again, you've shown yourself to be DIFFERENT and IMAGINATIVE through the use of one well-placed magic trick. Had you just walked up to the gentleman and started telling him how unique your company is, it might not have had quite the same effect. Telling your clients you're unique is one thing; showing them is something else!

TRADE SHOWS

Have a trade show coming up? Magic can be used in numerous ways to promote your product — ways that will grab potential clients and keep them at your booth. Imagine making your product float, appear out of nowhere, or vanish right before your clients' eyes. Once you've got their attention, you can use magic to demonstrate the benefits of your product as well! (Trick #23, for example).

Included in these pages are actual trade show magic tricks and sales presentations that I've put together and used in front of hundreds of people, and WHICH HAVE LEAD TO ACTUAL SALES! Now you too can perform these tricks, incorporating your product(s), and see firsthand the powerful response magic can generate.

TO ADD HUMOR

Any situation where you want to lighten up the atmosphere or cause someone to laugh is a great time to perform a trick. For example, business lunches, which can sometimes start off rather tense, can gently and humorously be loosened up through the use of magic. Imagine pulling a lit match from your pocket (Trick #4), to light your client's cigarette. Then imagine the look on her face when you cause her lit cigarette to vanish right before her eyes! (Trick #3).

Magic brings a smile to people's faces and a smile means they're having a good time — which can translate into better rapport between you and your customers.

NETWORKING

Magic can be used to open doors and help expose you to all kinds of interesting people. Whether you're at the airport, on a plane, at the doctor's office, or waiting for a taxi, you can use magic to make new friends, who will in turn introduce you to their friends, and so on. Pretty soon you have a whole new set of contacts that you never had before, thanks to some assertiveness and a few well-placed magic tricks.

Even something you do every day, such as handing out your business card, can be done with a bit of flair, using magic. Instead of just handing the client your card, why not make it appear at your fingertips? (Trick #1).

It's been said that nothing happens until somebody sells something. I hope I've sold YOU on the idea of adding magic to your arsenal of selling tools. If I have, then congratulations, you are about to learn how to SELL WITH MAGIC!

Michael Jeffreys

Los Angeles, California

PART I

THE PSYCHOLOGY OF SELLING WITH MAGIC

SELLING YOURSELF

The purpose of this book is to help you sell yourself better. With so many of today's leading companies offering the same products at approximately the same prices and competing for the same share of the marketplace, the entire success or failure of a company is virtually in the hands of its sales staff. Why? Because as products and services become increasingly similar (better, faster, cheaper), it is the salesperson who becomes the variable. It is he, through his actions or lack of them, who decides whether or not a product or service is purchased or passed over.

Anything you can do to make yourself special, different, or unique in the eyes of the customer is a step towards establishing rapport, and thus a step towards closing the sale.

The reason magic works so well in sales is that it helps break down many of those initial barriers that all salespeople encounter when first interacting with a client. After demonstrating one or two simple magic tricks, the prospect goes from thinking, "This guy is just trying to make a commission off me," to thinking, "This guy is a lot of fun; I'd like to listen to more of what he has to say."

If you've managed to tie in your product with the magic trick, then the customer will be all the more impressed that you were able to present your product or service in an entertaining and effective way!

MAGIC IS SELLING

Magic lends itself so well to sales because MAGIC is SELLING! You're selling the audience on an idea or situation that defies logic. Take the cut and restored rope trick for example. I doubt if anyone REALLY believes you can cause two pieces of rope to transform themselves back into one piece. However, if you've built the trick up properly and executed the necessary moves correctly, you can convince the audience that what they've just seen LOOKS impossible.

That's what a magician really is; a salesperson who sells the IDEA that he can do the impossible. The better job of selling he's done, the more the audience will be fooled.

Before a magician can sell a trick or effect to an audience, he must first sell himself. This means you must convince yourself of what it is you want the audience to believe. Imagine if you were to cut a rope in half, cause the halves to appear to go back together, then shrug your shoulders and quietly say to the audience, "Wow, isn't that the greatest thing you've ever seen?" Even if the audience DID think it was the greatest thing they'd ever seen, they would take one look at your reaction and think, "No, since you obviously don't think it is."

On the other hand, suppose you dramatically waved your hand over the rope while excitedly saying, "Now watch the two halves fuse back together into one single solid piece of rope." Then you proudly showed the rope back together, holding it up for everyone to see with a big, "See what I did, isn't that great" grin on your face. The audience would love it, and the applause would be forthcoming.

You've obviously sold yourself on the trick, and so the audience is more likely to buy what you're saying. Think about it. Aren't you more likely to buy something from a salesperson who really believes in his product, than from one who doesn't? Of course you are. Well, the same principle applies to magic.

KNOW WHAT THE EFFECT IS YOU'RE TRYING TO SELL

Ask any successful insurance salesman what it is he sells, and he will tell you, "security and peace of mind." Yet in reality, all he's really selling is a document that entitles the bearer or his family to a large amount of money should something happen to him. Now I'd like to ask you a question. From which insurance salesman would YOU be more likely to buy: the one who says that for x amount of dollars you can buy a piece of paper that says your family gets a sum of money if you die; or the salesman who assures you that, with a small investment, you and your loved ones will never again have to worry about the future? I think the answer is obvious. The second salesman would get the sale because he knows what the "effect" (benefit) is he's trying to sell — peace of mind, happiness, comfort, etc. and not simply a piece of paper!

The same thing applies to magic. You must be absolutely clear on exactly what the EFFECT is you're trying to sell. In the preceding rope trick, for example, you must know exactly what it is you want your audience to SEE and BELIEVE. Are you selling the effect that the two ropes have magically fused themselves back into their one original piece? Or are you selling the effect that the two ropes have vanished, and magically been replaced with one new long piece? While some would say the difference between those two effects is negligible, closer examination will reveal otherwise.

If the effect you wish to create is that the ropes are fusing themselves back together, then a logical step would be for you to rub the point of fusion with your finger tips, sort of "massaging" the ropes together. If, on the other hand, your intended effect was that of causing the ropes to vanish and be replaced by one new, long piece of rope, then obviously this sort of action would be completely out of place. Thus it is crucial that you are clear on what the effect is you wish to create so you can logically plan out all the steps you will need to take in order to arrive at that effect.

Furthermore, be sure that the effect you're trying to show the audience IS THE SAME EFFECT THE AUDIENCE BELIEVES THEY ARE SEEING. In other words, it is important that as you perform your magic, you make sure you and your audience are on the same wavelength.

Not being on the same wavelength as the person they are trying to communicate with is a problem that happens all the time to salespeople. For example, think of what typically happens to you when you go out to buy a new car. Instead of finding out what your needs are, the average car salesman hustles you over to his brand new 4 x 4, turbo, fuel injected, 18 cam, crashproof, fireproof, burglarproof, 180 mph barn burner, and tries to shove it down your throat. However, since all you're looking for is some cheap, reliable transportation, you're not the least bit interested.   All his enthusiasm about speed, aerodynamics, and rpm's has managed to do is turn you off.

The two of you were not on the same wavelength. The "effect" he was trying to sell wasn't the same "effect" you wanted to buy. As a consequence, the result was confusion, annoyance, irritation, lack of harmony, i.e. NO SALE!

In magic, if the performer isn't sure what he wants the audience to experience, they're probably not going to experience it! As you can see, understanding exactly what the effect is you're trying to sell is a prerequisite to performing magic.

WHAT MAKES A GOOD TRICK?

A good trick is one that can be easily followed by the audience. A trick that is too complicated or confusing probably won't fool anyone, and it certainly won't entertain them. Remember, if the audience has to stop and think about what you're doing, then they can't sit back and enjoy the magic.

A good trick is one that the audience can tell a friend about after the show, in one or two sentences. For example, "He made a lady float 8 feet off the ground!" or "He turned one dollar bills into fives right before my eyes!" are both tricks that are easy to follow.

However if the person says, "Well, he had me think of a number between 1 and 20, then he had me count that many down from the top of the a deck of cards, then memorize the card at that number, then shuffle the pack, then he caused the deck to become larger, then it became smaller, then it changed colors, and finally my card ended up inside a sealed envelope inside his wallet..." You get the idea. The effect, which is getting the selected card inside the envelope, has been muddled by all the other stuff going on.

I'm not saying you can't be creative. If you were to borrow a ring from a lady in the audience, cause it to turn into a turnip, then make the turnip vanish, then pull out a can of turnips, and using a can opener, open the can to find the lady's ring inside, that would be a great trick! I'm not even sure there is such a thing as canned turnips, but you get the idea. While there's a lot of magic going on here, the effect is simple: A borrowed ring ends up inside a can of turnips.

While the above premise is admittedly somewhat silly, it could make for a novel and interesting trick in the right hands. Why? Because the effect of making a borrowed object appear inside a sealed can is extremely strong. This leads us to our next topic:

SELECTING STRONG MATERIAL

Take a great actor, give him poor lines, and more often then not, you get a mediocre movie. Bill Cosby in "Leonard part six" is a perfect example of this. However, take an average actor, give him great material, and chances are you'll have a blockbuster. Sylvestor Stallone didn't win best actor for his performance in "Rocky," but the movie won best picture!

The same is true in magic. While you may not have the same amount of experience in performing magic as a Copperfield or a Henning, you can increase the strength of your magic performances by selecting strong material.

This means never performing any trick that leaves your audience saying to themselves, "Yeah, so what??" On the contrary, you want to perform the kind of magic that is going to knock their socks off!

To make your job as easy as possible, I've taken what I consider to be some extremely powerful and dynamic tricks, and literally placed them at your fingertips. Now it's up to you to go through the book and pick out those tricks from which you feel you can get the most mileage. I feel confident in saying that whatever tricks you end up performing, if you put in the necessary amount of practice, you will be more than satisfied with the results.

PRACTICING

Magic, like anything in life, requires practice if one is to become proficient at it. Obviously the more you practice the better you'll be. The question is, "How often should one practice?" While everyone is different, and some people just seem to pick up tricks faster than others, on the average you should practice a trick approximately 25-50 times before performing it in front of an audience.

While this may seem like a lot of rehearsing, believe me it isn't. Here's why: The first three or four times you run through a trick, you'll simply be getting used to handling the props in a manner that feels comfortable. This takes a little time. Most beginners in magic tend to handle magic props rather stiffly. This undoubtedly happens because they are worried the audience may detect that the box (for example) they are holding, which they claim is empty, isn't really empty. And so they get nervous and hold the box much more rigidly than they normally would. Only through practice is one able to train oneself to hold magic props in a relaxed and casual way.

On the next three or four run-throughs, you'll focus on performing the secret move or action that is necessary to make the trick work. Once you're able to physically do the move, your next three or four run-throughs will be spent on ironing out your execution of the secret move, so that you are able to perform it in a way that doesn't attract suspicion.

Let's stop here and take a look at how our little run-through is going. We've already practiced the trick nine to twelve times, and we haven't even worked out the talking or "patter" portion of the trick (patter is a term magicians use to refer to the dialogue they say while performing a trick). By the time you've practiced your lines and combined them with the trick, so that the whole routine flows together smoothly, effortlessly, and logically, you will have performed the trick well over 25 times!

I think you can see that practicing a trick CORRECTLY is a little more involved than you may have first thought. By the way, many magicians, myself included, will often practice certain moves to a trick literally hundreds of times in order to perfect them!

The good news is that all this practice pays off in spades when it comes time to perform in front of an audience. It gives you a feeling of confidence and leads to performing with precision! Dariel Fitzkee says in SHOWMANSHIP FOR MAGICIANS, "Precision comes with familiarity with your material, with utmost confidence in your ability, with exact knowledge of what you are to do and how to do it, and with the certain knowledge that when it is done your audience will like it."

Fitzkee also encourages the performer to "Cut every unnecessary thing out of the routine. Retain only the bare essentials to sell the idea." What we are talking about here is ECONOMY of motion and words. This means eliminating unnecessary movements and dialogue, taking out anything that could possibly confuse, distort, or muddle the audience's enjoyment and understanding of the trick.

PATTER AND TIMING

Patter refers to WHAT you say, timing refers to WHEN you say it. Jack Benny is acknowledged as the master of timing, and it is from him that we mere mortals can learn a thing or two about timing. Part of Jack's brilliance was that he developed a character with a flaw that everyone could relate to — stinginess. Thus he was able to elicit the longest nonstop sequence of laughter ever heard, over 5 minutes, simply by pausing to think when asked the immortal question, "Your money or your life?" He added another 2 minutes of laughter by replying to the robber, who was pressing him for an answer, "I'm thinking!"

Bob Hope, Red Skelton and Lucille Ball, themselves masters of comedy, shared the knowledge that timing can be the difference between a joke bringing the house down or getting groans.

My friend Bruce Gold, a comic who works Las Vegas regularly, has a wonderful example to illustrate the importance of timing. The line is: "I just finished a show in Las Vegas at the International House of Pancakes!" If you just read it straight through, you probably didn't think it was very funny. Now read it again with the proper timing: "I just finished a show in Las Vegas at the International... House of Pancakes!" See the difference a pause between International and House makes? You lead the audience down one line of thinking, that you just performed in Las Vegas, and then you surprise them by admitting it was only at a low priced restaurant.

Timing is a very difficult thing to teach. It takes the ability to listen carefully to a joke and see exactly where the humor lies. Then it takes the talent to deliver that joke in a way that conceals the humor from the audience until just the right moment. If you're a second too early or a second too late, the entire joke can be ruined or, at the very least, its impact weakened. That's why two comics can tell the same joke, and one can kill with it while the other only gets chuckles. One has the right timing; the other does not.

One way to develop timing is to tell a joke 10 times, emphasizing different words each time. For example, the old joke, "The other day I bet on a horse so slow, the jockey kept a diary of the trip!" should obviously be delivered with the emphasis on the words SO SLOW. If you emphasized any other words, the joke wouldn't be as funny.

If you try this "emphasis exercise" with any joke, eventually you will hit on a way of delivering the line that feels 100% better than all the other ways. You'll say to yourself, "Yes, that's it." Another way to improve your timing is by listening to other comics and hearing how they time their jokes. Remember, timing takes a while to develop, so don't get discouraged if it doesn't come right away.

Patter, on the other hand, can be improved simply by writing out what you want to say to the audience on a piece of paper. Once you've written it out, you can hone it, develop it, add jokes where you think you need them, etc.

Don't neglect your patter. Many magicians spend 80% of their time working on the technical part of their tricks, and only 20% of their time on the patter. This is a mistake. You should start off by spending 50% of your time on the technical aspects of the trick, and 50% of your time working out your patter. Then, once you've become proficient at the technical part of the trick, you will want to spend as much as 75% of your time on the presentation, and only 25% of your time keeping your technical skills sharp.

TRANSITIONS

To a magician, transitions refer to the time between tricks. A good transition keeps the momentum going from the previous trick and carries it right into the next one. However, since you will very likely perform only one trick for a group of clients before going into your sales presentation, let's define a transition as the time between the performance of a magic trick and the start of your "sales pitch."

Obviously you want your transitions to be as smooth as possible. Generally, you can tell the difference between a professional and an amateur by their transitions. When you AREN'T EVEN AWARE of the time between the trick and the beginning of the "sales pitch," the performer is obviously a professional and has made a smooth transition. Unfortunately, many performers don't spend much, if any, time on their transitions.

When you conclude a trick, and after the applause has subsided, you should ease directly into your sales presentation. There's no need to quickly shove the props from your last trick quickly into your pockets, as if you've got a plane to catch. Relax. If you've just amazed the audience with a well-presented trick, they will be with you.

The key to executing a good transition is to keep your attention ON THE AUDIENCE. If you do need a little time before going into your presentation, then tell a one-liner or make a remark about the trick you've just performed. Say anything, but don't drop your head and start mumbling, "Just a second, I just need to get this junk out of the way and then we'll continue..." Egad! Remember, the audience is the most important thing, so don't lose their attention, which you worked hard to get, by forgetting about them during the transitions.

MISDIRECTION

Misdirection is the technique magicians use to divert the audience's attention away from the secret of the trick. How important is misdirection? Without it, magicians would not be able to perform magic. Simply put, misdirection is the cornerstone of magic. When the magician pretends to place a coin into his right hand, but secretly retains it in his left, he MIS-DIRECTS you into believing the coin is in his right hand. He does this by holding his right hand as if it had a coin in it, looking at his right hand as if it had a coin in it, and just as importantly, NOT PAYING ANY ATTENTION TO HIS LEFT HAND, which in fact has the coin.

Think of misdirection as any action or statement the performer makes which is designed to conceal, or lead the audience away from the real modus operandi of the trick.

Misdirection also includes using nonverbal communication to help sell an effect. A gesture, a look, a raised eyebrow, even a pause can all be used to lead an audience down the wrong path. The only way to really become good at misdirection is by simply doing it. Work on focusing the audience's attention where YOU want it. When you can do this, and make it not look like work, you will have learned how to misdirect.

USING A MIRROR

Practicing in front of a mirror is one of the best ways to give yourself instant feedback as to how you look performing. By looking into a mirror, you can see pretty much how a trick will look from the audience's point of view. I say pretty much because a mirror only gives you a view from one angle, while an audience will be viewing you and the trick from many angles.

Watch your facial expressions too. You may think you are looking mysterious, when in fact you're really looking just plain silly. Many performers are amazed, after doing their act in front of a mirror, how little they smile. Keep in mind, your expressions should match your tone of voice. If they don't match, the audience will pick up on this and it will only serve to weaken your credibility.

Posture is another item that can be checked in a mirror.   You should always stand up straight, with your chest out and your chin up. This conveys an attitude of power. Never, never, NEVER slouch on stage!

FOCUSING ON THE AUDIENCE

During rehearsals, you should imagine how the audience will respond to what you're saying or doing. As you go through the trick, think to yourself, "Is what I'm saying interesting or am I putting the audience to sleep?" Put yourself in the audience and imagine if you saw a performer saying and doing the same things you're saying and doing; would you find it entertaining?

USING A VIDEO CAMERA

Probably the greatest machine invented in the last decade as far as the speaker, actor, magician or any other type of performer is concerned is the video camera. With the average price of most camcorders right around $1000.00, most professionals can and should own one. The feedback that a video camera can give you is incredible. Unlike a mirror, it gives you feedback from all angles. Unlike friends, it gives you honest, often brutally honest, feedback. And unlike film, it can be viewed instantly.

One of the things to look for, when viewing your tape, is where your eyes are looking. They SHOULD be looking directly into the camera, hard and fast. Your eyes should be engaging, mesmerizing, and full of life. Unfortunately, many performers have trouble making eye contact with their audience. This must be overcome if one is to be an effective magician.

A somewhat humorous, but nonetheless equally devastating mistake that many performers make is that they BLINK EVERY TIME THEY EXECUTE A SECRET MOVE! Somehow they think that if THEY don't see the secret move, the audience won't. A study of your practice tape will quickly reveal if you suffer from the "I can't bare to look" syndrome.

OVERCOMING STAGE FRIGHT

Every performer gets nervous before a show. Sweaty palms, heart palpitations, shortness of breath, flushed face, dilated eyes, and an abundance of energy are perfectly normal bodily reactions to performing in front of an audience. The question is not, will you suffer from these symptoms — practically all performers do to some degree — the question is, how will you deal with them?

If you "freak out" and become consumed with fear, then the stage fright has won and you will give a less-than satisfactory performance. However, if you retain your cool, stay calm, and learn to channel your "performance energy" (as I like to call it), you can actually use this energy to make you a more powerful and dynamic entertainer. Use it to project your voice, so that you can be clearly heard throughout the entire room or theater. Another way to channel this "performance energy" is to use it to keep you UP and ANIMATED throughout your presentation. As a performer, you should ALWAYS be exerting more energy then the audience, even if it's in a low key kind of way.

If however, you are so nervous just prior to going on that you feel out of control, the first thing you must do is get a grip on yourself. Breathing deeply 10 times just prior to going on stage can do wonders to help calm you down. Also, rising up and down on your toes will help release tension. Sometimes before a show I'll even jog in place. Jogging not only gets my mind off the show for a moment, it releases endorphins, which are natural chemicals that give the body a really good feeling (known also as the "runners high.")

The good news is that if you have properly rehearsed your material, once you step in front of the audience and start performing, the stage fright will begin to dissipate. In fact, after the first round of applause, the butterflies should practically be gone!

The bad news is if you haven't rehearsed properly the stage fright gets worse and worse, until minutes begin to pass like hours while on stage. Intense rehearsals will prevent occurrences such as this from taking place.

ORGANIZATION

Make sure when you perform your tricks, everything you need is easily accessible. If your pockets are cluttered with keys, coins, and other items not related to the trick, it's going to make it difficult for you to take your tricks out smoothly. It's a good idea to keep a pocket empty of all paraphernalia, except the trick itself.

Be sure you have all the props you'll need to perform the tricks AHEAD OF TIME. There's nothing worse then having to stop in the middle of a trick and say, "Excuse me, does anyone have a pen I can borrow?" — now the people around you have to start digging in their pockets and purses for a pen, and suddenly the flow of the trick has just come to a screeching halt. Had you asked ahead of time for a pen to be made available, or better yet, brought your own, this whole scene could have been avoided.

Your thoughts should also be well organized, so that there is no hesitation or breakdown in your movements. The last thing you want while you're performing is to look unsure of yourself. Practice will usually reveal how and where things need to be in order for the trick to flow smoothly.

WHAT TO WEAR

While the magician has traditionally donned a tuxedo while performing, in sales, the suit is the accepted form of attire. While the kind of suit you wear is obviously up to you, it should be appropriate to the audience you're addressing. If you're giving a presentation to a group of bankers, then a more conservative look would be appropriate. However, if you were doing a presentation for the National Dairy Farmers Association, then a less formal look would most certainly do the trick.

Probably the most important detail about a suit as far as a magician is concerned, is the number or pockets it contains. Pockets are to magicians what nurses are to doctors; they can never have enough of them. This is because, as I mentioned under ORGANIZATION, a magician only wants to keep one trick in each pocket. Anymore then this, and you risk the possibility of having to fumble around in the pocket, something you want to avoid at all costs.

Most men's suits tend to come with eight pockets: two side coat pockets, a breast pocket, an inside coat pocket for the wallet, and four pockets in the pants; two in the front and two in the back. Women's suits generally have fewer pockets then men's, however women have the advantage of being able to carry tricks in their purses. Yet even with both sexes having what would seem to be a lot of places to keep tricks, many men and woman magicians have pockets added to their favorite suits. This is so they can carry three or four close-up tricks with them at all times, and still have extra pockets for money, keys, etc.

These additional coat pockets are understandable when you consider that the pants aren't really the best place to keep magic. This is due to the fact that anything placed inside the rear pockets ends up looking like a pancake if the performer sits down (not to mention being excruciatingly painful.) Likewise, anything placed in the front pants pockets tends to get squished as well. Both sexes carry briefcases, which of course offers the most room for holding tricks. Ideally, you should have one carrying case just for magic; while keeping three or four of your favorite tricks in your "daily" briefcase.

ENTERTAINMENT VALUE

Entertainment value is what it's all about. It doesn't matter how well you perform a trick if the audience isn't entertained. That's why it takes so much practice to become good. Sure, you can learn the actual tricks themselves in one or two run-throughs. But to be able to perform the tricks in a way that entertains takes many hours of practice.

If I could give you one tip on how to make yourself more entertaining, it would be (other then focusing on the audience, which I already talked about), not to take yourself too seriously when performing. Nothing turns people off more then seeing a performer who thinks he or she is hot stuff. While the fact is you may be hot stuff, let the audience arrive at this conclusion on their own. There is something charming about a performer who is really good, AS WELL AS slightly humble. This doesn't mean you shouldn't present yourself with confidence, on the contrary, confidence is a quality you should ooze with. However there is a fine line between confidence and cockiness. The former wins an audience over; the latter turns them off.

Remember, magic is a tool through which to entertain — if the folks aren't entertained, no magic has taken place.

ATTITUDE

As a performer, you always want to keep an upbeat, positive, confident attitude. While you're performing your magic, or during the actual sales presentation, there should be no doubt as to who's in command. You want to come off as being sure of yourself without being condescending. In a sales situation, your clients will be looking at you for leadership. If they do decide to go ahead and purchase whatever it is you're selling, they will be studying you closely to see your reaction. If you look relieved, or have a grin on your face like the cat who just swallowed the canary, they will feel taken, even if it's only on a subconscious level. So be sure to compliment your customer on his or her smart buying decision. (After all, they must be smart if they just bought your product, right?)

Think about it. If you had just spent $600.00 for a brand new color T.V., wouldn't you feel even better about your buying decision if the salesman said to you, "Well congratulations, you just made an investment in a T.V. that I know you're going to love!"

ENTHUSIASM!

It's been said that nothing sells like enthusiasm. So get excited about your magic. Perform your tricks with a passion. Get off on them! Don't just say, "Want to see a magic trick?", say "Hey, watch this, this is really great!" If you really could make money appear out of thin air, or read someone's mind, wouldn't you be excited about it? You would say to everyone you meet, "Look what I can do, think of any number between 1 and 10 and I'll tell you what it is, this is really unbelievable..."

Enthusiasm is contagious. When people see that you're pumped up, they can't help but catch some of that enthusiasm themselves! If you're selling a product, it is then a matter of transferring the client's enthusiasm from your magic to the product.

FOUR EXCUSES

I want to take a moment before we get into the tricks to clear up four excuses I occasionally hear as to why some people hesitate to perform magic.

EXCUSE #1: I'M NOT VERY GOOD WITH MY HANDS

Having quick or graceful hands is NOT a prerequisite for being able to do magic. Proper execution of technique, knowing when and how to misdirect an audience, and being able to present a trick in an entertaining manner are what make a good magician.

Some of the best magicians that have ever lived had less than perfect hands for doing magic. Max Malini, one of the greatest magicians in the world during the early 1900s used to thoroughly baffle kings, queens, and presidents with his magic. Yet his hands were so small that when he would palm a card, the card would stick out from three sides of his tiny hand. Albert Goshman, a master of sleight of hand, started out as a baker. His thick, stubby hands which pounded out pizza dough for years, have earned him a small fortune making coins disappear at his finger tips and reappear underneath salt shakers!

So don't let the fact that your hands may not be mistaken for model's hands stop you from doing magic. If that ace card magician named Mcdonald was able to fool the best of 'em, and he had only one hand, you should have no problem with two!

EXCUSE #2: I DON'T HAVE TIME TO PRACTICE

While it's a good idea to set aside several hours a week to practice magic, there are lots of other ways to get in practice time. You can practice while watching T.V., in movie lines, at the doctor's office, while having lunch in restaurants, at the airport, and on airplanes (flight attendants love magic). In fact, since I usually carry a couple of magic tricks on me at all times, I find myself practicing whenever I have a few spare moments. I'm not saying YOU have to be that enthusiastic about practicing, but now you know why I smile when I hear people use the excuse, "I don't have time to practice."

By the way, the best way to practice the tricks in this book is to pick out four or five that you really like, then concentrate on really learning them until you have them down pat. Don't make the mistake of trying to learn every trick in the book. Remember, it's better to learn how to do five tricks well then 25 tricks poorly.

EXCUSE #3: MAGIC IS FOR KIDS

It IS for kids! The kid in me, the kid in you... the kid in everyone. Everyone likes to have his senses challenged, and that's what magic does; it makes people think. It's funny to watch different people's reaction to magic. Some people laugh at seeing something they can't figure out. Others get very serious and try to figure it out themselves. There's even a small minority of people who say they don't like magic because it upsets them, makes them feel stupid. That's okay too.

Why DO kids like magic so much? Because they're willing to let go of reality and pretend for a while. The kids know that the magician can't really float in the air, but they enjoy seeing something with their eyes that their minds can't believe. That's why magic is such good therapy for adults; it gets them to suspend their tight fisted grip on having to always be in control. It forces them to go back to being kids and letting the magic just happen. Thus magic serves not just as entertainment, but as a form of therapy. No, magic isn't just for kids, it's for everybody!

EXCUSE #4: I DON'T HAVE THE RIGHT KIND OF PERSONALITY TO DO MAGIC

What is the RIGHT kind of personality anyway? There are serious magicians, funny magicians, wry magicians, slapstick magicians, pompous magicians, cool-acting magicians, punk magicians, vaudeville-type magicians, cowboy magicians, tough guy magicians, and everything else in between. However, what you should strive to be is a good magician. And the way you do that is by BEING YOURSELF!

The very best magicians are those that are able to take who they are and project it to the audience through their magic. Thus, the better you know yourself, the more effective your magic will be. NEVER TRY TO COPY ANOTHER MAGICIAN. How on earth can you be a good magician if you copy someone else? It's impossible, because you know so little about how that person thinks and where he's coming from. Thus, while you may be able to copy most of his actions, you will never be able to capture the "essence" of who that person really is.

What you should do is sit down with a piece of paper and a pen, and write a profile of yourself. The profile should include your likes, your dislikes, how you think you come off to other people, etc. Once you've written this profile, ask yourself, "What would be the best way for a person with these traits to present his magic?" If you're a funny person who knows how to tell a joke, then obviously you would want to present your magic in a comedic way. If you tend to look at life in a somewhat serious manner, no problem, then present your magic in a serious way. The important thing is not to give up. Keep trying different ways of presenting your tricks until you find a way which you are comfortable with. Then fine tune that way until you're able to present your magic effortlessly. When you are able to do this, you will be a magician.

A Note About The Magician's Code

Since the beginning of magic, magicians have been reluctant to part with their secrets, since without them there would be no magic. It is therefore extremely important that you NEVER REVEAL THE SECRETS TO YOUR TRICKS, (or any magician's tricks for that matter). This may sound like a paradox since I'm divulging a number of magic secrets in this book, however this is not the case. Since you purchased this book, and the price you paid wasn't cheap, I assume that you are serious about learning magic.

On the other hand, to expose a secret to someone just because they ask, not only hurts all of magic, but greatly reduces your stature in that person's eyes. How? Because people generally give you quite a bit of credit for fooling them. After all, you did something they can't. If you tell them how you did it, they think, "Is that all there is to it? Heck, anyone can do that!" And so all you've succeeded in doing is taking away that wonderful feeling of mystery that you gave them a few minutes ago.

So what do you say when someone says, "How did you do that?" Well, you can come back with the stock reply, "Very well." Or you can do what I do: Simply smile and say, "If I tell you, then it won't be magic!" The reality is that most people don't really want to know how it's done anyway. So overcome the initial urge to comply with their request, and keep the magic a secret.

Sometimes people will ask you to repeat a trick a second time. Unless you're performing one of those special tricks that are supposed to be repeated, I recommend that you NOT repeat the trick. The reason is that the first time you do a trick, it's magic. If you repeat the trick a second time, the person concentrates on figuring out how you do it, and thus it becomes a puzzle, and is therefore no longer magic!

Getting The Most From This Book

You will have no trouble learning the tricks in this book if you take your time and don't rush. Resist the urge to simply read through all the tricks and see how they're done. Instead, start from the beginning and take each trick one at a time. If the trick appeals to you, gather up the necessary materials, and proceed with putting the trick together. Then learn the trick from the book WITH THE PROPS IN HAND. Trying to learn a magic trick from a book without having the necessary props is like trying to work out a math problem without pencil and paper... your mind eventually goes into overload, and frustration is usually the result. This, of course, is the last thing you want, so do take the time to gather the materials and make those tricks that you find appealing.

IMPORTANT: As you go through the tricks contained in this book, the question you should be constantly asking yourself is, "How can I adapt this trick or routine to fit what I market?" If the examples I use don't exactly fit your product or service, then change them so they do! THIS BOOK WILL BE OF NO VALUE TO YOU IF YOU SIMPLY READ THROUGH IT THINKING, "OH HOW CLEVER... ISN'T THAT INTERESTING."

WHAT YOU WANT TO DO IS THINK, "HOW DOES THIS APPLY TO WHAT I SELL? CAN I USE THE ENTIRE ROUTINE JUST AS IT IS? IF I CAN'T USE THE ENTIRE ROUTINE, ARE THERE PARTS OF IT I CAN USE? CAN I COMBINE TWO ROUTINES TOGETHER? HOW CAN I MAKE THESE MAGIC TRICKS WORK FOR ME?" If you think thoughts like these, you can't help but derive value from these pages.

As you're about to discover, magic can not only be used to entertain, but to motivate, captivate and persuade as well!

PART II

TRICK FORMAT DESCRIPTION

The format I use to teach the tricks in this book is as follows:

1) TRICK NAME — This appears underneath the TRICK #, and is the title I have given the trick.

2) QUOTES — Included with each trick is an uplifting or humorous quote.

3) COMMENTS — These are my comments, insights, and thoughts about the trick.

4) DESCRIPTION OF TRICK — This is a description of the effect: what you would see and hear if you were sitting in the audience watching someone perform the trick. (In some of the tricks "**Description of Trick**" precedes "**Comments.**")

5) THE SECRET — How the trick works.

6) MATERIALS — The materials you will need to make or perform the trick.

7) TO CONSTRUCT — How to make the materials into the trick.

8) SET UP — What you need to do just prior to performing the trick.

9) TO PERFORM — How to perform the trick while on stage. (Oftentimes I won't go into much detail on what to say under TO PERFORM, because I will have already told you what to say under DESCRIPTION OF TRICK.)

NOTE: Throughout the book, I refer to the person performing the tricks as "the performer," and to the client as "the spectator" or "the audience." This is to help remind you that you're not simply a salesperson who does magic tricks, but a complete performer who entertains, informs, and persuades.

To keep things simple, I have used the male gender (He/Him) throughout the text. I have done this, rather then continually switch back and forth between the male and female gender, purely for the sake of continuity. This should in no way be construed to mean that magic is strictly for men. It certainly is not. Magic can be performed equally as well or as poorly by either sex!

PART III

ICE BREAKERS AND COLD CALLING TRICKS

The tricks in this section are designed to be quick, direct, and exciting. They are for those times when you want to make a strong impression on a client and then move right into your sales presentation. By making a pen, coin, or lit cigarette disappear, you have grabbed the client's attention AND SHOWN YOURSELF TO BE DIFFERENT. You can now go into your sales presentation knowing you have the prospect's interest focused on YOU. (After making a lit cigarette disappear, who knows what you might do next?!)

Places you would want to perform these ice breakers include the clients office, your office, a business function, a restaurant, a party or other type of social function. Generally these tricks are designed to be performed for small groups, from one to six people.

By the way, the reason I've selected these particular tricks for this section on ICE BREAKERS AND COLD CALLING is that these tricks do not require the client to do anything but watch. If you're just meeting the client for the first time, it probably isn't a good idea to involve him in a lengthy magic trick right off the bat.

Thus the tricks are such that all the client has to do is sit back, watch, and be amazed! If he does express interest in your magic, you can use the magic as a means of forming rapport. If, on the other hand, he seems somewhat nonchalant about the magic, you simply don't have to make a big deal out of it. Just go into your presentation or continue your conversation.

The point is that there are no hard and fast rules when it comes to performing magic. You must be flexible enough to be able to change gears when the situation calls for it.

TRICK #1

THE APPEARING BUSINESS CARD

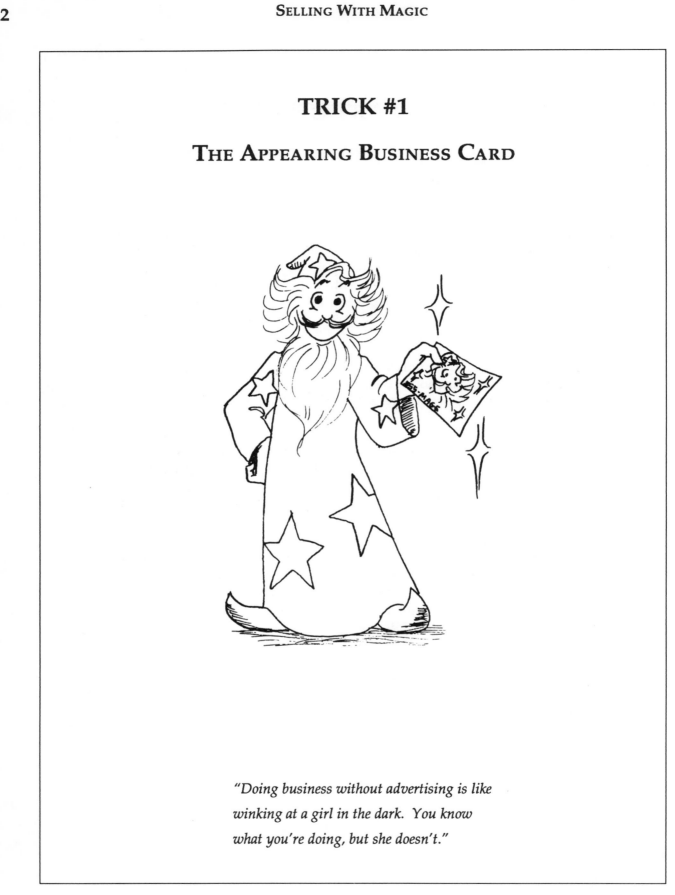

*"Doing business without advertising is like
winking at a girl in the dark. You know
what you're doing, but she doesn't."*

COMMENTS: I've decided to kick off the book with THE APPEARING BUSINESS CARD because often the first thing you do when meeting a prospective customer is hand him your business card. Once you've mastered this neat production of your card, you'll never again want to simply HAND your card to anyone!

DESCRIPTION OF TRICK: The performer reaches up into the air with an empty hand, and suddenly at his fingertips appears his business card!

THE SECRET: The card is secretly held behind the hand until it is brought into view in one quick flourish.

MATERIALS: A business card.

SET UP: To be able to produce the card, you must first get it into what magicians call, "back palm position." To do this, start with the card held in your right hand (assuming you're right handed) with your thumb on the face of the card, and your first and fourth fingers on the top and bottom of the card respectively (FIG. 1).

FIG. 1

The next step is for you to curl ALL FOUR of your fingers in, toward your wrist. The first and fourth fingers sort of curl over the top and bottom of the card, and along with the thumb, hold the card in place (FIG. 2).

FIG. 2

The next step is to straighten out your fingers, while simultaneously letting go with your thumb. The result is the card is now behind your hand, held between your first and second fingers and your third and fourth fingers (FIG. 3).

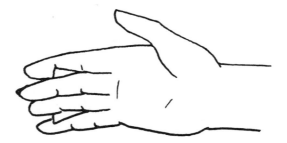

FIG. 3

If you straighten your fingers and hold them tightly together, you can make those pieces of card that are showing through your fingers all but disappear.

In essence, what you've just learned is how to make a business card DISAPPEAR! However that's not our goal. So, let's discuss how you're going to make the card appear from its current position, behind your hand.

Actually, all you're really going to do is REVERSE the previous three steps, but ALL IN ONE MOTION. In other words, once you have the card in position behind your hand, you're simply going to reach up into the air, curl your four fingers in, place your thumb onto the face of the card, and then straighten out all four fingers which leaves the card extending from your thumb and fingertips. Of course, when you actually perform the move, everything is done so quickly that all the spectator sees is, first an empty hand, and then a hand holding a business card. (FIG. 4).

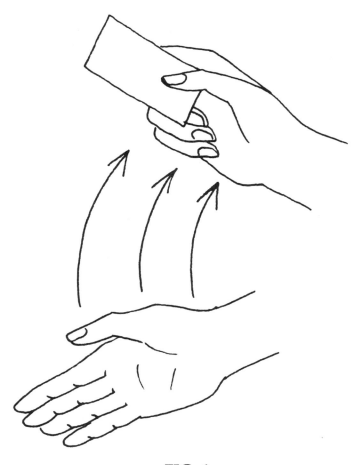

FIG. 4

Once the card is made to appear, you can curl your four fingers in, which is a more natural position than leaving them extended.

TO PERFORM: First get the card into "back palm position." Then walk up to the person you wish to make the card appear for and say, "Would you like one of my business cards?" Assuming he says, "yes," reach up into the air with your right hand, pause for a second, and then LOOK AT THE SPECTATOR AND THEN LOOK AT YOUR EMPTY RIGHT HAND. His eyes should follow yours to your right hand. This is a powerful nonverbal way for you to get him to look at your right hand without actually coming out and saying, "HEY, LOOK AT MY RIGHT HAND!" (After all, what good is making your business card appear if the person doesn't see it?)

Once you're sure the person is looking at your hand, say, "Here it is!" and reach up and pluck your business card out of the air. Freeze for a second after you've made the card appear to really let the visual image of what's just happened sink in. Then smile, and hand the person your card.

Obviously this trick will take practice, a lot of it in front of a mirror. Just don't give up, and before you know it, you'll be making your business card appear out of the air!

TRICK #2

THE VANISHING PEN

"In times of trouble, remember the steam kettle.

Though up to it's neck in hot water, it continues to sing."

DESCRIPTION OF TRICK: The performer takes out a normal looking Bic ball-point pen, and asks the prospect if she has seen these new "disposable" pens. When the prospect replies that she hasn't, the performer says, "They sure don't last long!" Suddenly the pen disappears right before the prospect's eyes!

COMMENTS: What makes the VANISHING PEN trick so powerful is that it really looks like magic. One second you're holding an ordinary pen and the next your hands are completely empty! This is one of my favorite tricks to perform for waitresses in restaurants. I just walk up to the waitress and say, "Excuse me, but did you drop this pen?" When she answers "No," I say, "Oh, sorry!" and then I make the pen vanish. You should see the look on her face! Believe me, it makes her day. I get a kick out of seeing her run back to her station and tell all the other waitresses what the "strange guy in the booth over there did!"

SECRET: Where does the pen go? Up the sleeve? No, actually the pen, which is attached to a piece of elastic, which is safety pinned to the inside back of your coat, flies inside your coat!

MATERIALS: A Bic ball-point pen with a cap, a piece of black elastic approximately 16 inches in length, a safety pin, and an ice pick.

TO CONSTRUCT: Take the ice pick and poke a hole in the pen cap (FIG. 1).

FIG. 1

Now take one end of the elastic, thread it through the pen cap and tie a couple of knots to keep the elastic from slipping through the cap (FIG. 2).

FIG. 2

Now attach the safety pin to the other end of the elastic (FIG. 3).

FIG. 3

Finally, attach the safety pin to the inside back of your coat, approximately 4 - 6" below shoulder level (FIG. 4). You're now all set to go.

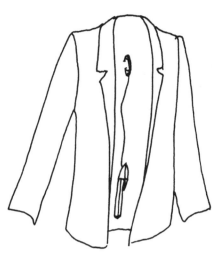

FIG. 4

TO PERFORM: The nice thing about this trick is that you can leave the pen pinned to the back of your coat and forget about it until you're ready to perform. When that time comes, simply reach back underneath the coat with your left hand, grab hold of the pen and bring it into view (FIG. 5). This should be done when the attention of the people you're about to perform for is elsewhere, and not on you.

FIG. 5

Be sure that when you bring the pen out, the elastic isn't hung up on the edge of the coat. You want the pen to have an unobstructed path to the inside of your coat.

Okay, so you're holding the pen in your left hand. Now, adjust your left hand so that it is only holding the cap of the pen. With your right hand remove the pen from the cap (FIG. 6), commenting on the fact that it is one of those disposable pens, etc.

PEN SHOOTS INTO COAT

FIG. 6   **FIG. 7**

Now place the pen back inside the cap TIGHTLY, and as you do so LET GO OF THE CAP and allow it, along with the pen, to shoot inside the left side of your coat (FIG. 7).

As long as the pen doesn't hit anything, like the edge of your coat or your stomach, it will come to rest behind you, underneath your coat. Immediately show your hands empty (FIG. 8).

FIG. 8

There is definitely a certain knack to performing this trick. Only by doing the trick over and over in front of a mirror will you be able to develop that knack. One tip I can give you is that if you are worried about the audience getting a glimpse of the pen shooting inside your jacket, you can clap your hands together as you let go of the pen. The larger motion of clapping your hands together will hide the smaller motion of the pen shooting inside your coat.

By the way, about the only way to make this trick more powerful is to use the spectator's pen. The way I do this is if I'm in an office and I see a Bic type pen lying on the table, I go into a corner, reach behind me and take hold of my Bic pen. Then I remove the pen and stick it in my inside coat pocket, leaving the pen cap concealed in my left hand. I then walk over to the person's desk and pick up their bic pen with my right hand. I make a comment about it, stick it into my pen cap which I have concealed in my left hand and OF WHICH HE IS UNAWARE, and make it disappear. When he asks me where it went, I just tell him it really disappeared!

At some point later, I'll retrieve the pen and secretly place it back on his desk without him seeing me. He usually finds it after I'm gone and I'm sure it gives him a good laugh.

TRICK #3

THE VANISHING CIGARETTE

"People who quit smoking cigarettes have the same problem as newcomers to nudist camps — they don't know what to do with their hands."

DESCRIPTION OF TRICK: The performer places a lit cigarette inside his fist. When he opens his fist, the cigarette is gone!

COMMENTS: The vanishing of a lit cigarette is one of the strongest tricks in all of magic. The following method is simple, direct and, best of all, you already have the necessary device with which to make the cigarette vanish.

THE SECRET: The cigarette goes inside the pen cap from the previous trick, THE VANISHING PEN, where it shoots inside your coat, leaving you free to show your hands empty.

SET UP: Assuming you've made up the elastic pen cap pull from the previous trick, simply remove the pen from the cap (place the pen in your pocket, as it is not needed for this trick), and you're all set to go.

By the way, if you haven't read the VANISHING PEN TRICK yet, I suggest you go back and read it before going on to this trick. In essence what you're going to do is instead of placing the pen into the cap, you're going to place a cigarette into the cap. The Bic brand pen cap is just the right size to wedge a normal size cigarette into (extra long "slim" cigarettes don't work).

Okay, with the pen cap pinned into position in the back of your coat, reach back with your left hand and secure the pen cap in your left fist. You, of course, do this just prior to performing the trick, when no one is looking. Casually drop your left hand to your side, while holding the pen cap in place with your 3rd and 4th fingers. You're now in position to perform the vanishing of a lit cigarette.

TO PERFORM: Ask to borrow a lit cigarette, taking it with your right hand. Bring your left fist up to approximately waist level, and SLOWLY lower the cigarette into your fist, LIT END FIRST. As it enters your fist, slowly guide the cigarette into the pen cap until you feel it wedge into place.

Let go of the cigarette with your right hand, leaving it sticking out of your left hand. Now two things are going to happen at once. You're going to let go of the pen cap with your left hand, and clap your hands together. The clapping of your hands together will help hide the vanishing of the cigarette. Again, as with the vanishing pen trick, be sure the pen cap has a clear pathway to inside your coat. Otherwise the cap and cigarette could get hung up on your coat or stomach, an occurrence that is extremely embarrassing.

Once the cigarette is gone, and you have clapped your hands together, slowly take your hands apart and show them to be empty. Believe me, the spectators will be astounded.

FINAL COMMENTS: There's no need to run to the bathroom immediately after performing the trick to remove the cigarette, as it quickly goes out once inside the pen cap. When you first try the trick, it is a good idea to start off with unlit cigarettes. That way if the cigarette accidentally comes flying out, you won't burn yourself, your clothes, or anyone who happens to be standing in the vicinity!

TRICK #4

LIT MATCH FROM POCKET

"Good salesmen, like good cooks, create an appetite where there was none."

DESCRIPTION OF TRICK: The performer is out having lunch with a client when he sees the client take out a cigarette. Without missing a beat, the performer reaches inside his jacket and removes a lit match! He then proceeds to light the client's cigarette.

COMMENTS: This trick is a little different from most magic tricks in that YOU don't decide when to perform the trick. The reason for this is that you must first wait for someone to come along who is in need of a lit match, and only then can you perform the trick.

In other words, if you were to just say to someone, "Hey watch this," and then proceeded to pull a lit match from your pocket, he would probably think, "Well, yeah that's cool." But on the other hand, if you were to wait until someone actually had need of match and then you casually reached into your jacket and came out with a lit match, then you would have something. Because not only did you do something amazing, but you did it just when it was most needed.

It's as if you and I were out taking a walk together and you casually mentioned that you were hungry, and suddenly I took off my hat and pulled out a tuna sandwich and handed it to you. Assuming you liked tuna, you would not only be blown away by the magic, but by the fact that I didn't make the sandwich appear until YOU mentioned you were hungry. The thinking being that had you not said anything, I would still be wearing that tuna sandwich on my head!

Well, you get the idea.

THE SECRET: A simple device consisting of a match striker, a safety pin, and a rubber band allows you to produce a lit match from just about anywhere.

MATERIALS: A book of matches, a rubber band, scissors, and a safety pin.

TO CONSTRUCT: Carefully cut out the match striker strip from the book of matches. Next fold the strip in half so that the sides with the striking surface are on the INSIDE. Now tear off a match and place it inside the folded strip. Next wrap the rubber band tightly around the strip, thus holding the match securely in place. Finally, place the safety pin through the top of the strip (FIG. 1).

FIG. 1

SET UP: While you can pin this striker device inside one of your pockets, I prefer to pin it inside my coat, on the left side (FIG. 2).

FIG. 2

TO PERFORM: Simply pin one or two loaded striker devices inside a few of your coats. Then next time you're out at a restaurant or bar and someone asks for a light, reach inside your jacket, grab hold of the bottom of the match and pull down sharply. The match should immediately light. If it does, nonchalantly pull it out and give the lady (or gentleman) a light. If it doesn't light, it could be one of three things: 1) The striking surface is worn out — I recommend you change them after every 10 lights, 2) the matches are too old — always using new matches will prevent this, or 3) the rubber band wasn't tight enough around the match head, and thus not enough friction was created to ignite the match. Try wrapping the band a few more times around the striker.

Because every once in a while a match will come out unlit no matter what you do, I recommend carrying a second loaded striker safety pinned right next to the first one. That way if the first match you reach for fails to light, you always have a backup.

TRICK #5

THE APPEARING FLOWER

*"All the flowers of all the tomorrows are
in the seeds of today."*

COMMENTS: This is not only an excellent trick for scoring points with the receptionist or secretary of an important client, but for impressing anybody of the opposite sex. Being handed a flower is one thing; having it made to magically appear for you is something else!

DESCRIPTION OF TRICK: Taking out a handkerchief, the performer opens it up and shows the spectator both sides. There is nothing on either side. Suddenly, the performer whisks away the handkerchief to reveal a beautiful rose, which he gives to the spectator.

THE SECRET: The flower is hidden inside the performer's coat, inside a special pocket. Under the guise of showing the handkerchief to be empty, the performer steals the flower from the secret pocket and loads it into the handkerchief. After appropriate fanfare, the flower is produced.

MATERIALS: A piece of black material, a box of safety pins, scissors, a non-see-through handkerchief (a cloth napkin works great), and a medium stemmed flower. (The flowers that work best are those with strong stems and whose petals have yet to fully open. The problem with using flowers that are in full bloom is that the petals fall off as you go to remove the flower from the secret pocket. The result is a rather wimpy looking flower.)

TO CONSTRUCT: Take the scissors and cut out a triangle measuring 10" x 10" x 5" from the cloth (FIG. 1).

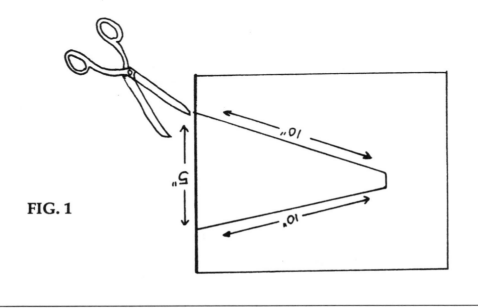

FIG. 1

Now safety pin the cloth to the left inside of the jacket you plan to wear when making the flower appear (FIG. 2).

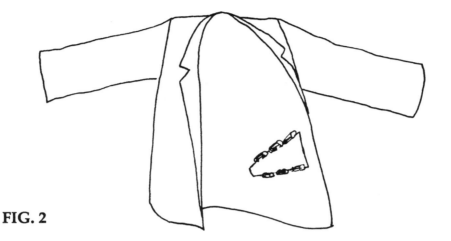

FIG. 2

SET UP: Put your jacket on, and then carefully slide the flower into the pocket, head first, leaving the stem protruding from the pocket. Ideally, the stem should come to approximately 1 - 2 inches from the edge of your jacket. (FIG. 3).

FIG. 3

Place the handkerchief inside your right outside jacket pocket and you're all set to go.

TO PERFORM: Take out the handkerchief and open it up so that your left thumb and fingers are holding the upper left corner of the cloth, and your right thumb and fingers are holding the upper right corner. Say to the person for whom you're going to make the flower appear, "Nothing here" (Fig. 4).

FIG. 4

You're now going to show the other side of the handkerchief empty by bringing your right hand to your left, in front of your left hand, and then draping the handkerchief over your left elbow (FIG. 5).

FIG. 5

Once the handkerchief is in place, it is now a simple matter to reach inside your coat, grab the protruding stem, and remove the flower. It is important that you do this WITHOUT LOOKING! Practice until you can just thrust your right hand into the pocket, grab the flower stem, and remove the flower. Once it is out of the secret pocket, hold the flower directly behind the handkerchief, out of sight of the spectator (FIG. 6).

FIG. 6

Finally, to reveal the flower, simply whisk away the handkerchief and then hand the spectator the flower.

FINAL COMMENTS: Be sure to hold your left arm up high (with the handkerchief draped over it), as you're reaching in to remove the flower with your right hand, so the spectator doesn't catch a glimpse of you making the steal.

You may have to adjust the position of the the secret pocket a few times before you find the angle that works the best, i.e., the one that allows you to remove the flower with the least amount of trouble. A few run-throughs will quickly reveal the correct angle.

TRICK #6

THE VANISHING COIN

*"Friendship is like money — easier made
than kept."*

DESCRIPTION OF TRICK: The performer causes a coin to vanish right before a spectator's eyes.

COMMENTS: One of my favorite ways to perform this trick is to walk up to a person with a quarter in my hand and say, "Excuse me, did you drop this quarter?" and when he says, "No, it's not my quarter," I smile and say, "Oh, I didn't think so," and then I open my hand and show him the quarter has vanished!

THE SECRET: A clever sleight known by magicians as "palming" is used to secretly retain the coin in your right hand, even though you appear to place it in your left hand.

MATERIALS: A quarter.

SET UP: While the trick requires no set up per se, you must first learn how to "palm" a coin. Although it does take a fair amount of practice to learn how to correctly palm a coin, once you have it down, you will be able to perform magic virtually anytime, anywhere.

I'm not making an overstatement when I say that palming is one of the most useful sleights in all of magic.

Okay, take the quarter (or if you have large hands, a half dollar) and with your left thumb push it into the palm of your right hand, just above the heel of the hand. Now remove your left thumb, but use the muscles in your right hand, the ones on both sides of the coin, to keep the coin in place (FIG. 1).

COIN "CLASSIC PALMED"

FIG. 1

Now turn your hand over. If the coin stays, you've palmed your first coin; if it falls out, you haven't.

Don't get discouraged if you aren't able to palm the coin right away. As I mentioned before, it will take a good amount of practice before you are able to keep the coin palmed in your hand WITHOUT LOOKING LIKE YOU'RE CONCEALING SOMETHING IN YOUR HAND. However, don't give up; the results are worth it.

The way I developed my palm was by carrying a coin around in the palm of my right hand for a week. Every time the coin would start to slip out of my palm, I would push it back in place with my left thumb. (By the way, if you happen to be left handed, then you'll obviously want to learn to palm with your left hand).

What happens is that after a while the muscles in your right hand learn to hold the coin in place. When you finally get it, it's a great feeling.

Okay, assuming you've put in the necessary practice and you know how to correctly palm a coin, let's go on to the next step, how to make the coin vanish.

TO PERFORM: Place the coin into your right palm, then walk up to the spectator and say, "Excuse me, did you drop this quarter?" As you say, "...drop this quarter," pretend to drop the coin into your left hand, but secretly palm it in your right (FIG. 2).

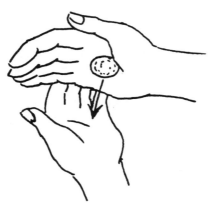

FIG. 2

Quickly close your left hand AS IF YOU'D JUST DROPPED A COIN INTO IT, AND EXTEND THE HAND TOWARD THE SPECTATOR. As you do this, casually drop your right hand to your side. At this point, it is extremely important that you LOOK AT YOUR LEFT HAND, as that's where the coin is supposed to be! Remember, the spectator will always look where you look (FIG. 3).

FIG. 3

Okay, so you've asked the spectator if the quarter belongs to him. When he says no, simply smile, open your hand and say, "Oh, I didn't think so." If you've performed the vanish properly, a look of bewilderment should appear on the face of the spectator. To make the coin reappear, simply reach behind the spectator's ear and produce the coin.

If on the other hand, you do not wish to make the coin reappear, then do the following: After you've pretended to place the coin into your left hand, say, "Look, if I just take this pack of gum..." Now reach into your right pants pocket, drop the coin, and remove a pack of gum. "And tap my hand three times with the gum, the coin vanishes." You can now open your left hand and show the coin has vanished, and both your hands are empty!

FINAL COMMENT: There is definitely a knack to making it look as if you really dropped the coin into your left hand. A good way to practice is to REALLY drop the coin into your left hand over and over, until you understand what that looks like. Then do the exact same motions, but this time palm the coin. If you did it right, it should look exactly like when you really dropped the coin into your hand. Only by practicing the sleight in front of a mirror many times will you truly be able to make the vanishing of the coin look like magic.

PART IV

SALES MEETING TRICKS

The tricks in this section are designed to emphasize a message rather than a product. The torn and restored $100 bill, for example, demonstrates the importance of quality in a product or service.   The $100 sign is a good trick for illustrating to your sales staff the importance of living in the present moment. The trick "Breakthrough!" is an excellent lead-in for a talk on overcoming obstacles.

Opportunities for performing these tricks include sales meetings, break-out sessions, motivational talks, sales presentations, and trade shows.

TRICK # 7

THE $100.00 SIGN

*In life, if you take care of the minutes,
the hours will take care of themselves."*

COMMENTS: This is an excellent trick for illustrating to your sales staff the importance of living in the present moment.

DESCRIPTION OF TRICK: Holding up a cardboard sign with a picture of a large CANCELED CHECK on it, the performer says to the audience, "We must learn to live for today, because the present is all we have. Yesterday is in the past; it's over and done with like this CANCELED CHECK." The performer turns the sign over and a picture of a large I.O.U. NOTE is seen. Continuing he says, "And tomorrow is an I.O.U for the future which is promised to no one."

The performer turns the sign over to the front again and the audience is surprised to see a large $100.00 BILL where the CANCELED CHECK was a moment ago. With a smile on his face, the performer says, "That's why we must learn to live in the present, because only today is REAL SPENDABLE CASH!"

THE SECRET: A secret flap on one side of the sign makes this effect possible.

MATERIALS: A sheet of thick white cardboard (at least 1/16th of an inch thick), three sheets of thin black poster board (almost like paper), a can of 3M spray-on adhesive, a roll of black electrical tape, scissors, a large picture of a canceled check (simply enlarge one of your own checks on a copying machine and then write CANCELED across it), a large $100.00 bill (available at most joke shops), and a large I.O.U., which you can draw by hand.

TO CONSTRUCT: Cut the piece of thick white cardboard down so it measures 15 1/2" high x 17 1/2" wide.

Cut out two pieces of black cardboard that measure 16 1/2" wide x 14 1/2" high. Now cut out a third piece which measures 16 1/2" wide x 7 1/4" high.

Using the 3M spray adhesive, carefully coat one side of the white board and one side of one of the two larger pieces of black cardboard with glue. Wait one minute and then place the black cardboard, coated-side down, in the center of the white board, which is coated-side up. You should now have a black sign with a 1/2" white border.

Repeat the above step with the second piece of large black cardboard, gluing it to the other side of the white cardboard. Let dry.

Now take the remaining piece of black cardboard (the one measuring 16 1/2" x 7 1/2"), and lay it on top of the black piece of cardboard you just glued on so that it lines up flush with the bottom of the black cardboard. Now use the electrical tape to tape the top of the piece of cardboard down, thus creating a flap (FIG. 1).

TAPE ALONG DOTTED LINE!   **FIG. 1**   SECRET FLAP   **FIG. 2**

Next, with the flap in the UP position, carefully glue the picture of the CANCELED CHECK on the front of the sign (FIG. 2).

Now put the flap down and glue the large $100.00 bill onto the sign (FIG. 3).

FIG. 3   **FIG. 4**

Finally, turn the sign over and glue the I.O.U. picture on the back (FIG. 4).

And there you have it, your very own "$100.00 sign!"

TO PERFORM: Hold the sign at approximately chest level (so as not to block your face), with your fingers holding the secret flap up so the CANCELED CHECK can be seen by the audience. After talking about how yesterday is spent like a canceled check, flip the sign over so the I.O.U. is now facing the audience. As you talk about how tomorrow is like an I.O.U. that's promised to no one, slip your thumbs underneath the flap and push it up so the hidden sign, the $100.00 bill, comes into YOUR view UPSIDE DOWN, (the audience is still looking at the I.O.U.) As soon as you get the flap up, turn the sign over so the $100.00 bill is now facing the audience. As you do this, comment on how only today is real "spendable cash", and so we should strive to live in the present moment as much as possible!

At this point the trick is over and you can set the sign aside and go into your presentation.

FINAL COMMENTS: The fact is, ANY short message can be relayed to your audience in a magical way using this sign with a hidden flap concept. Here are a few more ideas to help get your creative juices flowing:

Let's say you're speaking before a large corporation, for example, The Century 21 Real Estate Company. You could hold up the sign to show a competitor's name and say, "Some people think that ABC real estate is the best (turn the sign over and lift flap), and some think XYZ real estate is the best (another competitor), but WE know the company that truly leads the way in the real estate field is (turn sign over and show) CENTURY 21!"

Or, if there is a particular person you wish to acknowledge during your speech, like the president of the company, for example, here's how you do that: Hold up the sign with a picture of Abraham Lincoln and say, "Here is a president who was a GOOD leader." Turn the sign over and show a picture of John Kennedy and say, "Here is a president who was a GOOD leader." And here is a president who is a GREAT leader, (Lift flap and turn sign over) YOUR PRESIDENT, MR. KARL NEWMAN!" (Show picture of company president).

Remember, you're only limited by your imagination... which means you're not limited at all!

TRICK #8

THE TORN AND RESTORED $100.00 BILL

*"A man is a failure who goes through
life earning nothing but money."*

COMMENTS: This a great trick for selling any product or service, since it emphasizes quality and receiving full value for your money.

DESCRIPTION OF TRICK: Holding up an obviously fake $100.00 bill, the performer says, "Don't be fooled by cheap imitations; some products may look good from a distance, but upon closer examination you will often find them to be less then what they claim." He then proceeds to tear the fake bill into pieces. The audience can clearly see separate pieces of bill. After folding the torn pieces into a packet, the performer says, "At XYZ industries, our products are guaranteed to be 100% genuine, to do all the things we say they'll do, or your money back." The performer then slowly opens up the packet, and much to the amazement of his audience, he is now holding a brand new, GENUINE, $100.00 bill!

THE SECRET: Affixed to the back of the fake $100.00 bill is a real $100.00 bill. During the tearing of the fake hundred, the two bills are switched.

MATERIALS: A new GENUINE $100.00 bill, a fAKE $100.00 bill (available at any toy store), and a bottle of rubber cement.

TO CONSTRUCT: Place the GENUINE $100.00 bill on a flat surface and carefully "accordion pleat" the bill into six equal sections (FIG. 1).

FIG. 1   **FIG. 2**

Next turn the bill 90 degrees and then fold it into thirds by folding over 1/3 of the bill from the left side and then 1/3 of the bill from the right, creating a small packet (FIG. 2).

Now apply a coat of rubber cement to the "bottom" of the packet and glue it to the back of the FAKE $100.00 bill, in the top left corner (FIG. 3). Place a book over the bills and let set until the glue has dried.

FIG. 3

SET UP: Place the bill(s) inside your wallet and you're all set.

TO PERFORM: Take out your wallet and remove the FAKE $100.00 bill, while holding the GENUINE bill with your left thumb to keep it from opening up prematurely (FIG. 4).

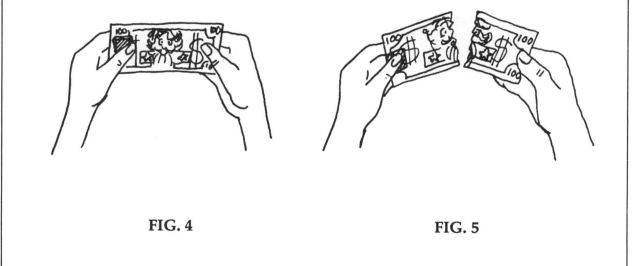

FIG. 4   FIG. 5

By the way, if you want to show the back of the fake bill before you start to tear it, here's how you do it: First let go of the right side of the bill with your right hand and use your right fingers to cover the genuine bill. Now, in one continuous motion, turn the bill around so the audience can see the back, KEEPING YOUR FINGERS OVER THE GENUINE BILL. After a beat, turn the bill back around by reversing the movement.

You have just shown both sides of the bill. Since the audience has no idea of what it is you're going to do, there is no need to worry that they will suspect anything. Just be natural.

The next sequence is the tearing of the bill. Start by tearing the bill down the middle (FIG. 5).

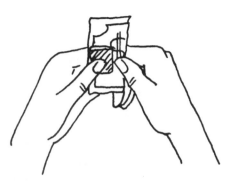

FIG. 6

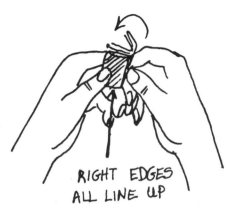

RIGHT EDGES
ALL LINE UP

FIG. 7

Hold the torn off right half of the bill up for the audience to see; then place it IN FRONT OF THE LEFT HAND HALF. Now tear the bills again down the middle; hold up the pieces in the right hand for all to see, and then place them in front of the pieces in the left hand once again.

You are now holding four "pieces" of $100.00 bill in your left hand with the piece closest to you having the genuine $100.00 bill attached to it (FIG. 6).

Fold the right side of the torn bills in towards the middle of the packet, so that the newly formed edge lines up with the right side of the genuine bill (FIG. 7).

Now fold the left side of the bills into the middle so that the newly formed left edge lines up with the left side of the genuine bill. Now fold the top of the torn bills down and the bottom of the torn bills up.

When you are finished you should have two packets, EXACTLY THE SAME SIZE, stuck to each other. At this point the torn bill is still facing the audience, and the genuine bill is still facing you (FIG. 8).

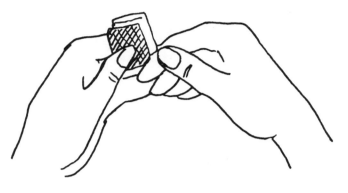

FIG. 8

All that is left to do now is turn the packet over and open up the genuine bill. Obviously you don't want to just turn the bill over and start opening it up; that would look suspicious. What you do is turn the packet over under the guise of blowing on the bills. As the right thumb and first finger take the packet from the left thumb and first finger, the move is done. More specifically, as the right thumb and first finger approach the packet to take it, the right hand turns PALM UP, thus your right thumb goes in front of the packet and your fingers behind it. Now as you bring the packet to your lips to blow on it, it is a natural action to simply revolve your right wrist towards you, which in turn revolves the packet (FIG. 9).

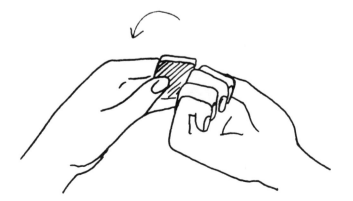

FIG. 9

After you have blown on the bill(s), and in the process turned over the packet, slowly open up the front genuine bill. Because you accordion pleated the bill, it should open up quite easily. Keep your left thumb over the torn pieces on the back of the bill to keep them from falling.

If you wish, you can show the back of the bill. However, if you do, remember to keep the pieces covered with your fingertips.

Finally, fold the bill in half with the torn pieces going inside the bill, and begin your sales presentation.

TRICK #9

CHANGING ONES INTO FIVES

*"Money can't buy love, health, happiness,
or what it did last year."*

COMMENTS: This is a great trick with which to open a sales meeting because it's quick, direct, and extremely visual. In addition, the message that the trick illustrates is a key concept in sales.

DESCRIPTION OF TRICK: The performer says to his audience, "The nice thing about sales is that your income is directly connected to how hard you work. If you don't work very hard, your commissions won't be very big." The performer removes five $1.00 bills from his billfold, which he shows on both sides. Next he says, "But if you decide to work hard and put out the necessary effort, your commissions will multiply accordingly." He then blows on the bills and they instantly change into $5.00 bills!

SECRET: A "gimmicked" bill with a secret flap makes this trick possible.

MATERIALS: Five $1.00 bills, five $5.00 bills, and a bottle of rubber cement.

TO CONSTRUCT: To make up the gimmicked bill, take one of the $1.00 bills and fold it in half so there is a crease running through George Washington's picture. Now take one of the $5.00 bills and fold it in half so there is a crease running through Lincoln's picture.

Now place both bills on the table FACE UP and apply rubber cement to the RIGHT HAND side of the $1.00 bill and to the LEFT HAND side of the $5.00 bill (FIG. 1).

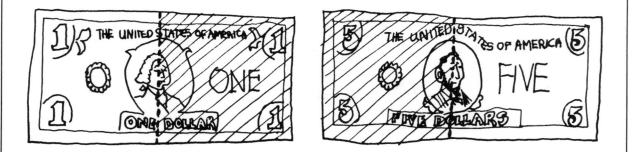

FIG. 1

Before the cement has a chance to dry, take the $5.00 bill and place it FACE DOWN on top of the FACE UP $1.00 bill. Place a book on top of the bills and let dry.

When you are done you should be left with a bill with a "flap." When the flap is closed, you are looking at the back of a $5.00 bill and when the flap is open, you see half a $1.00 bill and half a $5.00 bill (FIG. 2).

FIG. 2

Take the remaining four $5.00 bills and fold them in half so there is a vertical crease running down the middle of Lincoln's picture. Insert these four bills, PICTURE SIDE UP, underneath the $5.00 half of the flap (FIG. 3). Once the $5.00 bills are inside, push the flap all the way down against the bills.

FIG. 3

Next take the gimmicked bill and turn it over so the back of the $1.00 bill is now face up. Hold this packet in your left palm with your left thumb keeping the loose $5.00 bills in place against your palm (FIG. 4).

FIG. 4   FIG. 5

Take three of the remaining $1.00 bills and place them face down on top of the gimmicked bill.   Place the last remaining bill face down underneath the stack (FIG. 5).

Now fold the bills in half toward yourself, and then place a money clip (or any type of clip) over the folded bills to keep them in place. Place the bills in your left jacket pocket and you're all set.

TO PERFORM: After talking about how the amount of money you can make in sales is directly tied into how hard you work, take out the clipped bills, holding them in your left hand. Use your right hand to remove the clip and place it in your pocket. Using your right thumb, peel back the $1.00 bills into view, one at a time, as you count out loud, "One, two, three, four, five $1.00 bills (FIG. 6)."

FIG. 6

Next count the bills again, taking them ONE AT A TIME with your right hand from your left. Place each bill UNDER the next one as you count them, thus reversing their order "One, two, three,..." As you count "four," TAKE ALL THE BILLS AND THE GIMMICKED BILL TOGETHER AS ONE. As you count "five," turn the last bill over a couple of times and let the audience see both sides. Place this last bill ON TOP of the stack.

Square all the bills and place them back into your left hand with the left thumb holding the hidden $5.00 bills in place once again. Fold down the top of the bills toward you, your left thumb lifting just enough to allow the folded bills to go underneath it. Once the bills are underneath, the thumb clamps back down, holding everything in place.

Say to the audience, "But if you decide to work hard, your little commissions will turn into big ones, just as these $1.00 bills turn into $5.00 bills!" As you say this line, grasp the outer end of the packet and flip it towards you, so that half of a $5.00 bill is now showing (Fig. 7). This takes place as you bring the bills up to your mouth to blow on them.

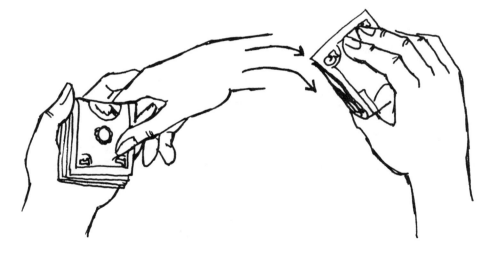

FIG. 7

Next take the bills with your left hand and peel the $5.00 bills back to show each one. At this point it helps if you grab the fives and reposition them in your left hand so the hidden packet of ones is securely held in place by your left thumb.

You can now take the top four $5.00 bills and show them with your right hand, while retaining the gimmicked bill with the ones inside of it in your left hand (Fig. 8).

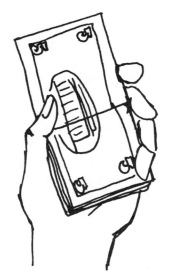 

FIG. 8

When you're finished showing the $5.00 bills place the fives in your right hand on top of the gimmicked five in your left hand and fold the packet in half.

To finish, take out the clip from your pocket, put it on the bills and put the clipped bills back in your pocket. You now have the perfect lead in to talk about the proverb, "As you sow, so shall you reap," as it applies to sales.

TRICK #10

BREAKTHROUGH!

"The reason a lot of people can't find opportunity is that it is often disguised as hard work."

COMMENTS: This is an excellent trick to use as a lead in for a talk on how every worthwhile goal requires the overcoming of obstacles, many of which at the time seem insurmountable.

DESCRIPTION OF TRICK: Holding up a handkerchief with the word GOALS written on it, the performer says, "While having goals is crucial if one is to be successful, there are always going to be obstacles that get in the way of achieving those goals.

The performer stuffs the handkerchief inside a glass, which he says will represent an obstacle or barrier. He then covers the top of the glass with a second handkerchief and secures it with a thick rubber band, thus trapping the goals handkerchief inside the glass.

The performer then states that any goal can be reached if one wants it badly enough. With that he proceeds to pull the goals handkerchief right through the bottom of the solid glass, without disturbing the second handkerchief or the rubber band!

SECRET: Sometimes the most mind boggling tricks involve very simple solutions, as this trick illustrates. The secret lies in the fact that you turn the glass containing the goals handkerchief upside down as you cover it with the second handkerchief. Thus what the audience thinks is the top of the glass is actually the bottom. It is then a simple matter to reach under the outer handkerchief and remove the goals handkerchief from the glass. (The hardest part of the trick is keeping the GOALS handkerchief form falling out too soon!)

MATERIALS: A clear glass, two handkerchiefs (one white and one colored — any color), a thick rubber band, and a black marker.

TO CONSTRUCT: Using the black marker, write the word GOALS in large letters across the front of the white handkerchief. If you tape the scarf down flat on a table before you write, the letters will come out straight and wrinkle free (FIG. 1). (It is a good idea to put newspaper underneath the handkerchief to prevent the ink from bleeding through and ruining your table.)

FIG. 1

SET UP: Roll the GOALS handkerchief into a tube and place it inside the glass. The colored handkerchief goes inside your left coat pocket and the rubber band inside your right coat pocket. You're now all set to perform BREAKTHROUGH!

TO PERFORM: Remove the handkerchief from the glass and unroll it so the audience can clearly see the word GOALS. Say, "We all know how important it is to have goals in life. Yet no matter how carefully we've planned out our goals, there are bound to be some obstacles that pop up along the way."

"These obstacles or barriers can be overcome, however, if one is determined enough." Holding up the glass, say, "This glass will represent a barrier." Stuff the goals handkerchief inside the glass in such a way that if the glass were turned over, the handkerchief would NOT fall out.

Hold the glass in your right hand, BY THE TIPS OF YOUR RIGHT FINGERS AND THUMB, as your left hand takes out the colored handkerchief from your pocket. Say, "To make the glass escape proof, I will seal off the top of it with this blue (or whatever color you're using) handkerchief."

Bring the handkerchief up in front of the glass, temporarily blocking the audience's view of the glass (FIG. 2).

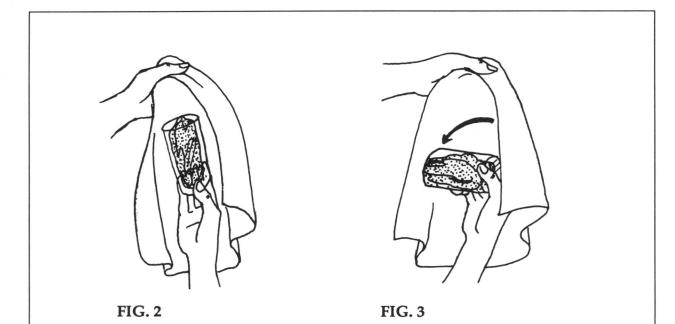

FIG. 2   **FIG. 3**

As you begin to cover the glass with the handkerchief, your right hand RELAXES its grip on the bottom of the glass, causing the top to swing downward (FIG. 3).

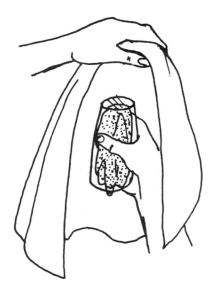

FIG. 4

When you have completed this secret move, the mouth of the glass will be pointing towards the floor (FIG. 4).

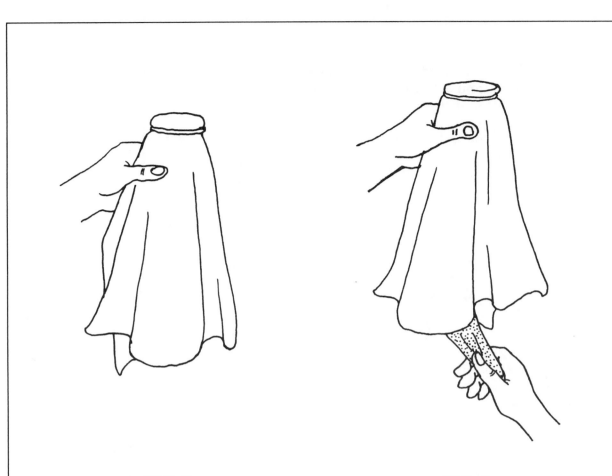

FIG. 5   **FIG. 6**

You see why it is important to stuff the handkerchief inside the glass securely — so it doesn't fall out when you perform the secret move. The whole move only takes a split second to perform. To the audience it should merely look as if your left hand placed the handkerchief over the glass.

Once the glass is covered, grip it through the handkerchief with your left hand. With your right hand take out the rubber band and place it around the top of the glass (FIG. 5). (This is the bottom of the glass, but the audience believes it to be the top.)

THE PENETRATION: You're now going to appear to pull the goals handkerchief right through the bottom of the glass by reaching under the colored handkerchief and into the glass with your empty right hand. Grab a corner of the GOALS handkerchief and slowly start pulling down on it, extracting it from the glass. Be sure to pull it straight down so it looks as if it's penetrating the bottom of the glass (FIG. 6).

As you do this say, "And yet as impossible as it seems, the handkerchief melts through the bottom of the glass like a knife through butter." (Try it in front of a mirror, it looks so real you might even fool yourself!)

Once you pull the entire handkerchief out, open it and display it to the audience. Next reach underneath the colored handkerchief with your right hand and grip the mouth of the inverted glass (FIG. 7).

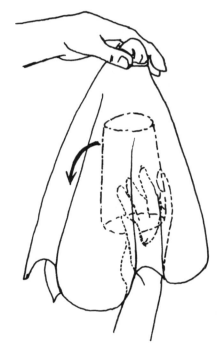

FIG. 7   **FIG. 8**

Now repeat the secret move of letting the glass swing down between your right finger tips and thumb (FIG. 8).

At the same time as the right hand is letting the glass swing down, the left hand is pulling the handkerchief and rubber band off the top (really bottom) of the glass. Important: As the left hand pulls the colored handkerchief and rubber band away it must PAUSE FOR A SECOND to give the right hand a chance to perform the secret move. Once the move is completed, continue pulling the handkerchief away, thus bringing the glass into view exactly as it should be, mouth up (FIG. 9).

FIG. 9

You are free at this point to hand out all the props for examination.

TRICK #11

HOW TO MAKE THOSE LITTLE SALES PROBLEMS DISAPPEAR!

"Disguised inside every problem is an opportunity."

DESCRIPTION OF TRICK: The performer holds up a glass filled with colored confetti. He states that the confetti inside the glass represents the multitude of annoying little problems that the average salesperson faces each day in his life; things such as making phone calls that clients don't return, running late to appointments, finding out a client never received the packet you mailed, etc.

After this introduction, the performer covers the glass with a handkerchief — the outline of the glass can be clearly seen through the material. The performer states, "In order to be successful, we must learn how to handle those little annoying worries and problems... or better yet, make them disappear!" Suddenly the performer throws the covered glass up in the air, whereupon the glass of confetti instantly vanishes, leaving nothing but an empty handkerchief to float back down to the performer's empty hands!

THE SECRET: You actually ditch the glass long before tossing the handkerchief into the air. A round disc sewn inside the handkerchief creates the illusion that the glass is still under the handkerchief until the moment it disappears.

MATERIALS: Two identical handkerchiefs (or cloth napkins), a glass, a piece of thick cardboard, scissors, masking tape, a black felt tip pen, a shoebox, three thumb tacks, two brass fasteners, a bag of confetti, a table, a table cloth, a couple of rags, and access to a sewing machine.

TO CONSTRUCT: Lay the glass mouth down on the piece of cardboard. Use the black marker to trace a circle around the edge of the glass. Take the scissors and carefully cut around the outside edge of the circle so that the newly formed disc will be slightly larger than the mouth of the glass (FIG. 1).

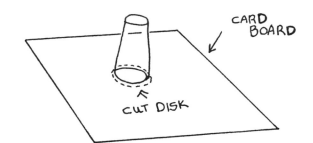

FIG. 1

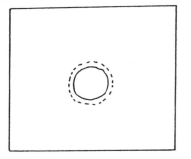

FIG. 2

Next take the disc and sew it to the center of one of the handkerchiefs (FIG. 2). Now take the second handkerchief and lay it over the first handkerchief and sew it around the edges (FIG. 3). Thus you now have a fairly thick handkerchief with a disc concealed in the center.

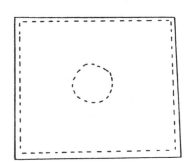

FIG. 3   **FIG. 4**

Take a piece of masking tape, write the word "PROBLEMS" on it and stick it on the front of the glass. Now fill the glass 3/4 full of confetti (FIG. 4).

Cut two little strips of cardboard (each piece should be approximately 3" long x 1" wide) and, using the brass fasteners, attach these strips to the box (FIG. 5)

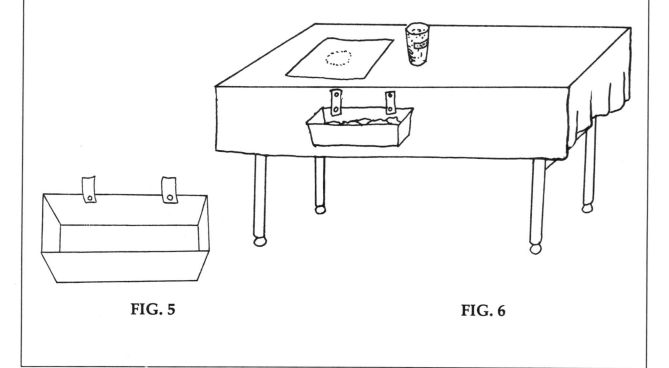

FIG. 5   **FIG. 6**

SET UP: Place the tablecloth over the table you will be using. Next, place the rags inside the bottom of the shoe box, and then use the thumb tacks to hang the shoe box from the back of the table (FIG. 6). (Be sure the tablecloth is large enough to prevent the audience from seeing under the table and discovering the shoe box).

Place the handkerchief and glass on the table and you're all set to go.

TO PERFORM: Hold up the glass as you tell the audience that the confetti inside the glass represents the multitude of annoying little problems that all salespeople face every day of their lives. Comment how wonderful it would be if we could all learn how to handle our problems in a quick and efficient manner. Cover the glass with the handkerchief making sure that the disc goes over the top of the glass (FIG. 7).

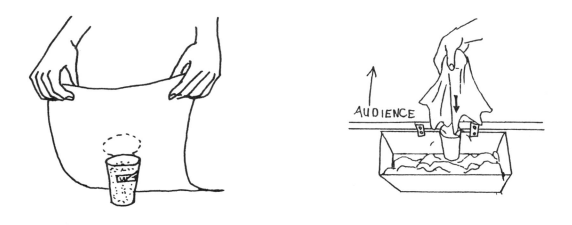

FIG. 7   **FIG. 8**

Pick up the handkerchief covered glass and bring it back over the rear edge of the table. Then loosen your grip on the glass allowing it to fall into the shoe box (FIG 8).

Be sure that when you let go of the glass, the handkerchief is touching the top of the table, so as to provide cover for the falling glass. The rags will muffle the sound of the glass hitting the bottom of the box.

Because you're holding the disc through the material, the audience still believes the glass is under the handkerchief. Bring the handkerchief forward, away from the table as you say, "Or better yet, wouldn't it be wonderful if we could learn to make our problems disappear!" As you say "...disappear," throw the handkerchief up in the air. As it comes down, catch it, open it up, and show both sides to be empty. Smile and take your bows.

FINAL COMMENTS: The act of covering the glass, picking it up off the table and throwing it into the air should be ONE SMOOTH MOTION. There should be no hesitation or jerky movements as you drop the glass. Practicing in front of a mirror is crucial to performing this trick successfully.

As you've probably already surmised by now, the method used to make the glass of confetti vanish can also be used to make other small objects vanish. Items such as a can of coke, a can of oil, a small box of cereal or cookies, a box of toothpaste, etc. can all be made to vanish via a secret cardboard shape hidden between two handkerchiefs. Next time you're giving a presentation to your co-workers, why not make the competition's product disappear?

TRICK #12

TURNING PROBLEMS INTO SOLUTIONS

"Having problems may not be so bad after all. There's a special place for folks who have none — it's called a cemetery."

COMMENTS: This trick is a visual way for you to show potential clients that you and your company are interested in coming up with solutions to whatever problems they may be having.

DESCRIPTION OF TRICK: The performer, who is addressing a group of potential clients, holds up a napkin with the word PROBLEMS written on it in large letters. He crumples the napkin into a ball as he says, "We here at XYZ Inc. are confident that if you give us your PROBLEMS, and just a little bit of TIME..." The performer takes out a watch and touches it to the rolled up-napkin, "We can come up with the right SOLUTIONS!" He opens up the napkin and it now says "SOLUTIONS" on it in large letters!

THE SECRET: You switch the PROBLEMS napkin for the SOLUTIONS napkin when you reach into your pocket to take out the watch.

MATERIALS: Two identical paper napkins, a black marker, a roll of masking tape, a watch, and a piece of newspaper.

TO CONSTRUCT: Tape the newspaper down onto a table. Next fold back 8 pieces of tape (so they are sticky on both sides) and place 4 pieces underneath each napkin, thus securing the napkins to the newspaper. Write the word PROBLEMS on one napkin, and the word SOLUTIONS on the other in large black letters (FIG. 1). (The newspaper prevents the ink from bleeding through onto the table).

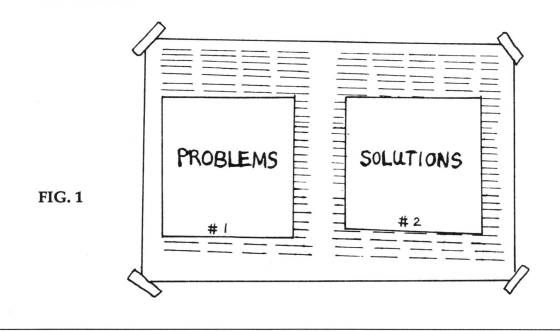

FIG. 1

Carefully remove the tape from the napkins.

SET UP: Crumple up napkin number two, with the word SOLUTIONS on it, into a ball, and place it in your right pants pocket. Then fold up napkin number one, with the word PROBLEMS on it, and place it in your left pants pocket. Place the watch into your right coat pocket and you're all set to go.

TO PERFORM: After talking about problems in business, reach into your right pants pocket with your right hand and secretly palm the crumpled-up napkin (fig. 2). (Palming is a magicians term which means to hide an object in your hand without your audience knowing it's there.) If you do this casually, without making a big deal out of it, no one will suspect a thing. Remember, no one has any idea what you are about to do.

AT THE SAME TIME your right hand is palming out the balled up napkin, your left hand reaches into your left pants pocket and takes out napkin number one. Unfold this napkin so the audience can see the word PROBLEMS written across it. As you do this, be sure to keep ball number two hidden in your right hand (Fig. 3).

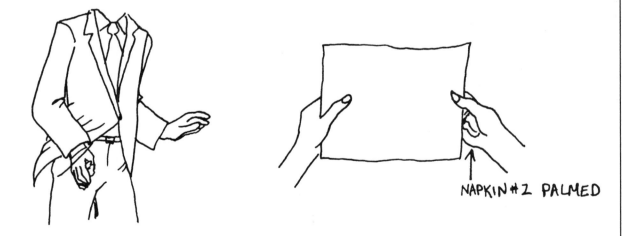

NAPKIN #2 PALMED

FIG. 2   **FIG. 3**

Now say, "We at XYZ Inc. (or whatever your company is called) are confident that if you give us your PROBLEMS..." and then begin to crumple napkin number one into a ball. Again, be sure to keep your right fingers close together so the audience doesn't see the palmed napkin (Fig. 4).

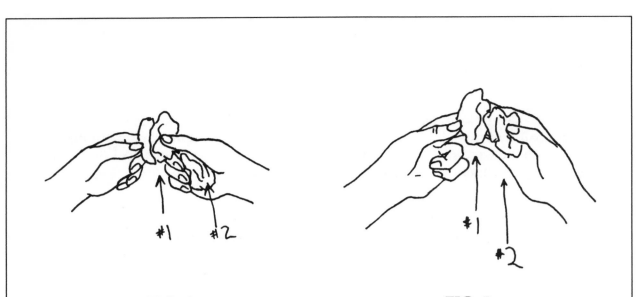

FIG. 4   FIG. 5

You are now going to switch napkin number one for napkin number two.
Here's how: With your left hand push napkin number one on top of napkin
number two, and squeeze both napkins together (Fig. 5). Immediately take the
napkins from your right hand with your left hand and hold them up. Be sure
that napkin number one stays in front (Fig. 6).

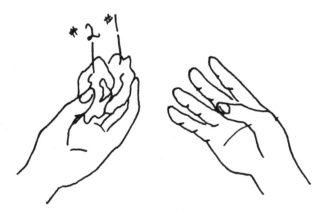

FIG. 6

To the audience, it appears as if you are merely showing them the crumpled-up
napkin. As you display the balled up napkin(s) with your left hand, hold up
your right hand and show it empty.

You are now going to place the napkins back into the right hand, but as you do, you are going to switch the two napkins by rotating your left wrist a 1/4 turn clockwise (FIG. 7). This allows you to place the napkins into your right hand with napkin number TWO GOING ON TOP, and napkin number one going underneath it (Fig. 8).

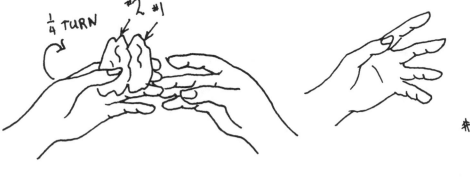

FIG. 7   **FIG. 8**

Show your left hand empty and reach into the top of your right hand, removing the top napkin, napkin number two, leaving behind napkin number one, palmed in your right hand. THIS COMPLETES THE SWITCH. While it takes quite a few words to describe the move, it only takes a few seconds to perform it. Okay, you've just done the switch. The next move is to get rid of the napkin in your right hand. Here's how: While still holding up napkin number two in your left hand, place your right hand into your right outside coat pocket. Drop the ball in the pocket, grab the watch and bring it out.

Unbeknownst to your audience, you have just cleverly gotten rid of the PROBLEMS napkin right under their noses. Touch the watch to the balled-up napkin in your left hand as you say, "and just a little TIME, we'll find the right SOLUTIONS!" All you have left to do now is slowly and dramatically open up the napkin and show the word SOLUTIONS on it.

TRICK #13

THE VANISHING RED SCARF IN DOLLAR BILL

*"Time wasted thinking up excuses would
be better spent avoiding the need for them."*

COMMENTS: This is a good trick for illustrating how your product can save the prospect both time and energy.

DESCRIPTION OF TRICK: After borrowing a one dollar bill from a spectator, the performer removes a 9" red silk scarf from his pocket. The performer says to his audience, "This red scarf represents your time and energy. This dollar bill represents your hard earned money." The performer rolls the borrowed dollar into a tube and then proceeds to push the silk scarf slowly, without any tricky moves whatsoever, into the rolled-up dollar bill. The performer says, "Many times we go through life spending all our time and energy trying to make money. Yet when everything is said and done, we having nothing left to show for it." The performer unrolls the dollar bill, and the audience is amazed to see that the scarf has vanished! The performer shows both sides of the bill, but there is no sign of the scarf.

The performer then slowly rolls the empty dollar back into a tube. Then he says, "The key is to invest your money wisely so you have MORE TIME AND EN-ERGY to do the things that really matter to you." He then reaches inside the dollar and, to the amazement of the audience, pulls out the red silk scarf! The performer goes on to explain how his product can save the prospect both time and energy.

THE SECRET: A magician's gimmick called a thumb tip makes this visual miracle possible. The silk scarf actually goes inside the thumb tip (which you secretly placed inside the dollar bill as you were rolling the bill into a tube), and is then stolen out of the bill by your right thumb where it stays hidden until you are ready to make the scarf reappear.

(Warning: While the thumb tip is available in many children's magic sets, it is nonetheless one of the magician's most powerful tools. I've included it in this book only because there is no better way to make a scarf disappear and then reappear than with a thumb tip. However I must ask that you keep the thumb tip a secret from non-magicians (as you should all the secrets in this book), so magicians can continue to fool the public with this powerful gimmick.)

MATERIALS: A Vernet thumb tip — available from any magic shop (This magician's prop is simply a hollowed-out plastic thumb that is worn over your real thumb). You also need a red 9" square silk scarf which, like the thumb tip, is available at most magic shops. You can, of course, make your own scarf by going to a fabric store and buying a piece of 9 1/4 inch red silk and hemming the edges yourself.

SET UP: Place the thumb tip in your right pants pocket and the scarf in your left pants pocket, and you're all set to go.

TO PERFORM: Place your right hand into your right pants pocket and slip the thumb tip onto your right thumb. AT THE SAME TIME, your left hand reaches into your left pants pocket and takes out the red scarf.

Ask to borrow a dollar bill (you could use your own, but the effect is stronger if you use a borrowed bill). Take the bill with your left hand, which is still holding the scarf, and wrap it around your right thumb (and thus the thumb tip as well) (FIG. 1).

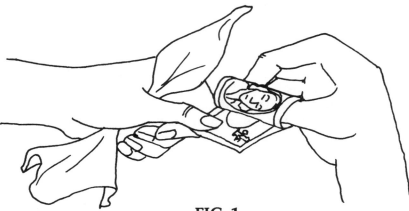

FIG. 1

Next pull the newly formed "tube" off your right thumb with your left fingers, and take the scarf with your right hand (FIG. 2).

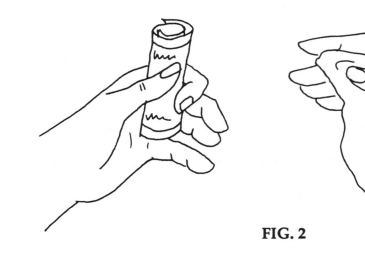

FIG. 2

Slowly push the scarf into the bill and into the thumb tip with your right first finger. Use your right thumb to help pack down the scarf into the bill. It is as you are pushing the last few inches of scarf into the bill that your right thumb jams itself into the thumb tip. When you feel the thumb tip securely on your right thumb, casually withdraw your thumb from the bill, taking the "loaded" thumb tip with you (FIG. 3).

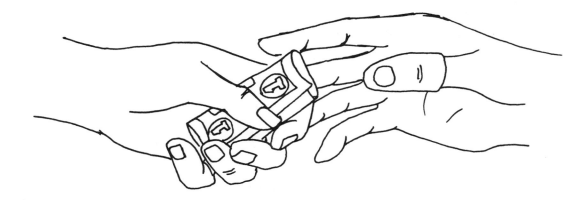

FIG. 3

Now slowly and dramatically unroll the bill and show the audience the scarf has vanished. Turn the bill over a couple of times to show both sides. Don't worry about the audience seeing the thumb tip. As long as the people watching you perform are more than a few feet away, they won't see a thing. Remember, their eyes are looking for a 9" red scarf, not a flesh-colored plastic thumb.

To make the scarf reappear, simply roll the dollar around your right thumb again, and then pull your thumb out of the bill, leaving the "loaded" thumb tip inside the bill. Now show your right hand empty and, reaching into the bill, slowly remove the scarf. Believe me, you will get a great response from the audience with this trick.

Once you pull the scarf all the way out of the dollar, nonchalantly stick your right thumb inside the bill, allowing the thumb tip to jam onto your thumb. Now withdraw your thumb from the bill taking the tip with it. This whole move takes only a second.

Now unroll the dollar and hand it back to the person who loaned it to you (be sure to thank him). As you do this, casually place the scarf inside your pocket, getting rid of the thumb tip at the same time.

FINAL COMMENTS: For what to say while you're performing, you can either use the dialogue I've provided in TRICK DESCRIPTION or come up with your own.

This is one of my favorite tricks and one that I perform quite often because the thumb tip and scarf are so small that they fit nicely inside my pocket. Thus wherever I go I always have this neat little "eye popping" trick which I can perform anytime, anywhere. (And so can you if you take the time to get the necessary props!)

PART V

NETWORKING TRICKS

The tricks in this section are designed to involve the spectator in the magic. Thus instead of just sitting back and watching the magic, as with the tricks in the ICE BREAKERS section, you are actually involving the prospect in the trick. In essence you are "networking" him into the trick.

Obviously some of the tricks from the ICEBREAKERS section can and should be used for networking, and vice-versa.

Ideal places for performing these tricks include restaurants, seminars, workshops, people's homes, sales meetings, hospitality sweets, etc.

TRICK #14

THE FLASH APPEARING BUSINESS CARD

*"If you want to be the picture of health,
you'd better have a happy frame of mind."*

COMMENTS: This is another version of trick #1, THE APPEARING BUSINESS CARD, the difference is that this version is a little flashier and involves the prospect.

DESCRIPTION OF TRICK: Taking out a lighter and a piece of paper, the performer hands the lighter to the prospect requesting that he light the paper. Upon being lit, the paper immediately bursts into flames. The performer reaches into the flames and magically produces his business card which he hands to the startled prospect!

SECRET: The performer has the business card palmed in his right hand, unbeknownst to the prospect. After the paper, which is called "flash paper" and is chemically treated, is lit by the spectator, the performer simply reaches into the flames and produces the palmed card at his fingertips.

MATERIALS: A 4" X 4" piece of flash paper (available at most magic shops, flash paper sells for around $4.00 an envelope — each envelope contains four large sheets).

Also needed are a business card and a lighter.

SET UP: Place the business card and the lighter in your right jacket pocket and the flash paper in your left jacket pocket and you're all set to go.

TO PERFORM: Reach into your right jacket pocket with your right hand and palm the business card as you simultaneously remove the lighter (FIG. 1).

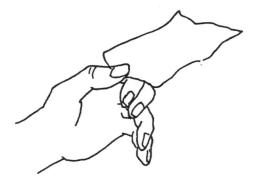 

FIG. 1

At the same time as your right hand is palming the business card and bringing out the lighter, your left hand reaches into your left jacket pocket and takes out the piece of flash paper (FIG. 1).

Hand the lighter to the spectator with your right hand (which still has the card palmed.) Hold the edge of the flash paper with your left fingertips and ask the spectator to light the paper. As the paper is being lit, you must quickly reposition your fingers in order to get the business card in the correct position to make it appear. This "get ready" only takes a second, but it must be practiced so it can be performed smoothly. The first step is to bend the first finger BACK, BEHIND THE CARD. The second step is to bend the second finger inward so that it is pressing tightly against the card (FIG. 2).

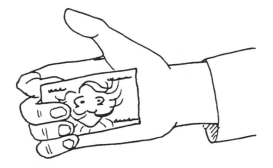

FIG. 2

That's it — that's the get ready. The card is now being held by your first and second fingers, ready to be produced.

Okay, the prospect has started to light the paper, you've performed your get ready, and now the paper is burning away. Since flash paper burns extremely quickly, you've got to move fast. AS YOUR LEFT HAND LETS GO OF THE BURNING PAPER, your right hand reaches up about an inch from the flame, and then you EXTEND YOUR RIGHT FIRST AND SECOND FINGERS. This will automatically bring the business card into the flame. As the flame disappears, the business card will become visible to the prospect (FIG. 3).

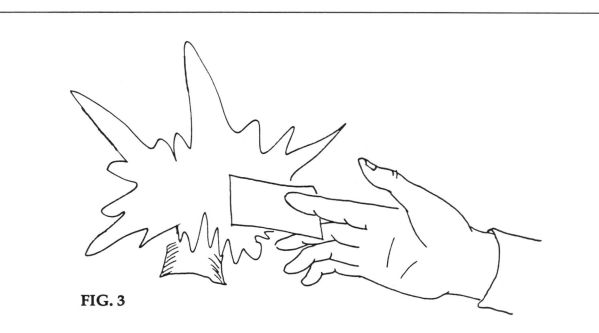

FIG. 3

Done with the proper timing, the appearance of the card can be made to look most magical. Once you've made the card appear, you should change your two-fingered grip on the card to a more natural position. To do this, place your thumb on the back of the card and move your first finger to the front of the card (FIG. 4).

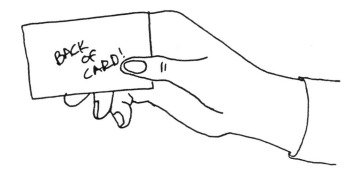

FIG. 4

Hand the card to the spectator with the knowledge that he will never forget you and the magical way you made your business card appear for him!

IMPORTANT WARNING: FLASH PAPER CAN CAUSE SEVERE BURNS IF MISHANDLED OR IMPROPERLY USED. IN FACT, EVEN WHEN PROPERLY USED, THERE'S ALWAYS THE CHANCE THAT SOMEONE COULD GET BURNED. ALWAYS LOOK AROUND YOU BEFORE PERFORMING THIS TRICK TO SEE IF THERE'S ANYTHING THAT COULD CATCH FIRE, SUCH AS A WOMAN'S HAIR OR THE TOP OF A LITTLE CHILD'S HEAD.

THE AUTHOR, PUBLISHER, AND ANYONE ELSE CONNECTED WITH THIS BOOK TAKE ABSOLUTELY NO RESPONSIBILITY WHATSOEVER, NOR CAN OR WILL THEY BE HELD LIABLE FOR ANY INJURY CAUSED BY THE USE OF FLASH PAPER, WHETHER IT'S TO THE PERFORMER OR TO A SPECTATOR.

Please take the above warning seriously. A number of years ago I was performing in front of about 2000 people and, because of the sweat on my hand, I had an entire sheet of flash paper, which I had just lit, stick to the palm of my hand! The four-letter words that came flying out of my mouth at that moment don't even begin to describe the pain I was in. So take my advice and be extremely careful when using flash paper.

TRICK #15

WHAT COLOR IS YOUR BUSINESS CARD?

*"The best way to appreciate your job is
to imagine yourself without one."*

DESCRIPTION OF TRICK: The performer places four of his business cards in a row in front of the spectator. He points out that each card has a different colored sticker on it: red, blue, yellow, and green.

The performer hands a book of matches to the spectator and asks him to select any one of the four colors he would like by placing the matchbook on the color of his choice.

The spectator (for example) chooses red. After offering the spectator a chance to change his mind, the performer says, "I knew you would choose red." He then reveals a prediction that has been sitting on the table throughout the trick. The prediction reads: YOU SELECTED RED.

This trick is foolproof and works every time.

COMMENTS: This is a great trick for anyone in business because, not only do you perform a nifty bit of magic for the spectator, but you also leave him your business card. Every time he looks at your card he will see the colored sticker and be reminded of the amazing trick you performed for him. Don't be surprised if he asks you how you did it, to which you smile and say, "Why it's magic, of course!"

THE SECRET: The fact is you actually have four different predictions, one for each color, cleverly hidden in the props with which you are working. Thus no matter which color is chosen, you are able to reveal a prediction that names his color as the one that will be selected! (Some tricks are so sneaky it's all you can do to keep from breaking out into a big grin while you're performing them!)

MATERIALS: Four of your business cards, four round colored stickers — red, blue, yellow, and green, each about the size of a dime (the kind used for pricing merchandise), a plastic business card case, a sheet of blue and a sheet of black colored stick-on letters, a piece of white cardboard a little smaller then the size of a business card, a book of matches, and two felt-tip pens: one green and one red.

TO CONSTRUCT: Place a sticker onto each business card (FIG. 1).

FIG. 1

Remove an X from the sheet of black plastic stick-on letters and place it on the back of the business card with the YELLOW sticker on it (FIG. 2).

FIG. 2

Now remove the letters B L U E from the sheet of blue stickers and place them on the back of the business card case (FIG. 3).

FIG. 3

Using the red felt tip pen write: YOU SELECTED RED on the piece of white cardboard and insert this prediction into the side of the business card case opposite the clear plastic window (FIG. 4).

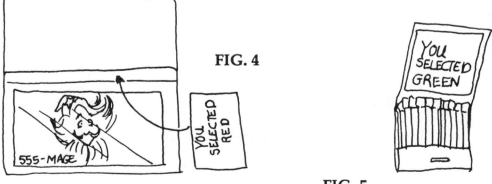

FIG. 4

FIG. 5

Now take the green felt-tip marker and write on the inside of the matchbook: YOU SELECTED GREEN (FIG. 5).

Finally, place the four business cards, colored-sticker side up, into the side of the card case with the clear plastic window. Place the business card case along with the closed up matchbook into your pocket and you're all set to go.

TO PERFORM: Take out the business card case and remove the four business cards and lay them in a row in front of the spectator. Set the card case down on the table, near the cards. BE SURE NOT TO FLASH THE BOTTOM OF THE CARD CASE AS YOU ARE DOING THIS; THE SPECTATOR MIGHT GET A GLIMPSE OF THE WORD "BLUE" ON THE BOTTOM OF THE CASE AND THIS OF COURSE WOULD SPOIL THE TRICK.

Now take out the book of matches and hand them to the person requesting he place them on any one of the four colors he would like. Tell him that he has an absolutely free choice as to what color he selects and that it makes no difference to you (which it doesn't!).

Depending on which color the spectator chooses, here is what you do:

1) If the spectator places the matches on the business card with the GREEN sticker, simply say, "Would you please look inside the matchbook." Upon opening the matchbook he will be amazed to read, YOU SELECTED GREEN.

2) If the spectator places the matches on the business card with the BLUE sticker, say, "I knew you'd select blue and I can prove it," and then turn over the business card case and show him it says BLUE on it.

3) If the spectator places the matches on the business card with the RED sticker, say, "I made a prediction of the color you'd select and placed it inside the card case." Pick up the card case, hold it open for the spectator and allow him to reach inside the card case and remove the piece of cardboard with YOU SELECTED RED written on it. The reason you hold the card case is to prevent the spectator from turning the case over and discovering the word BLUE written on the bottom.

4) If the spectator places the matches on the business card with the YELLOW sticker, casually lift off the matches and say, "I knew you'd select yellow... would you please turn over the card you selected." He will be amazed when he sees the black X on the back of the card, however he will be even more amazed when he turns over the other 3 cards and finds nothing on the back of them.

While he is busy turning over the other cards, you have ample time to casually place the book of matches and the card case into your pocket, thus getting rid of the evidence.

Remember, the whole key to this trick is to act as if whatever prediction you reveal, is THE ONLY PREDICTION YOU HAD. If the spectator even suspects that you have more than one prediction, the trick is ruined. It is only by doing the trick a number of times that you will learn how to best sell the prediction that matches the selected color.

It should be obvious, but I'll say it anyway: THIS TRICK DEFINITELY CANNOT BE REPEATED FOR THE SAME AUDIENCE. The very nature of the secret of the trick precludes this. However, you may be asked by the spectator to repeat the trick. What do you do? Well WHAT I DO is smile at him and say, "I could, but then you'd be twice as frustrated as you are now!"

TRICK # 16

THE CHEAP RUBBER BAND

"Creativity starts by stretching the mind in new directions."

COMMENTS: This quickie never fails to get a strong reaction. Whenever I'm in an office, I love to go over to the secretary or office manager and perform this trick for her.

DESCRIPTION OF TRICK: Walking up to the office secretary, the performer asks her if she has a rubber band he may have. Taking the rubber band from her, he begins to stretch it between his hands until suddenly, "snap," the band breaks into one long useless piece of rubber. As the secretary starts to reach for a new rubber band, the performer says, "Wait, watch..." SUDDENLY THE RUBBER BAND IS SEEN TO VISUALLY RESTORE ITSELF BACK INTO ONE CONTINUOUS LOOP! The performer hands the restored rubber band back to the amazed secretary for examination.

THE SECRET: The rubber band is never really broken; a clever bit of handling just makes it appear as if it breaks apart.

MATERIALS: A rubber band.

TO PERFORM: Ask to borrow a rubber band from the person for whom you wish to perform (try to get a thin band, as thick ones don't work as well). Take the band from her and as you do, look her in the eye and say, "Oh, do you have the time?" The moment she looks down at her watch, perform phase one of the trick, THE SET UP: First pinch the left end of the band between your left thumb and first finger, then pinch the right end of the band between your right thumb and first finger. Pull the band taut between your hands (FIG. 1).

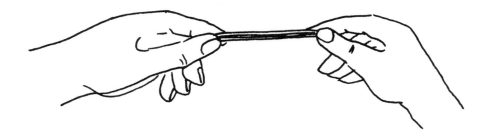

FIG. 1

Next wrap the band around the bottom of your right hand, bring it up behind your hand and then between your right thumb and first finger (FIGS. 2A & 2B).

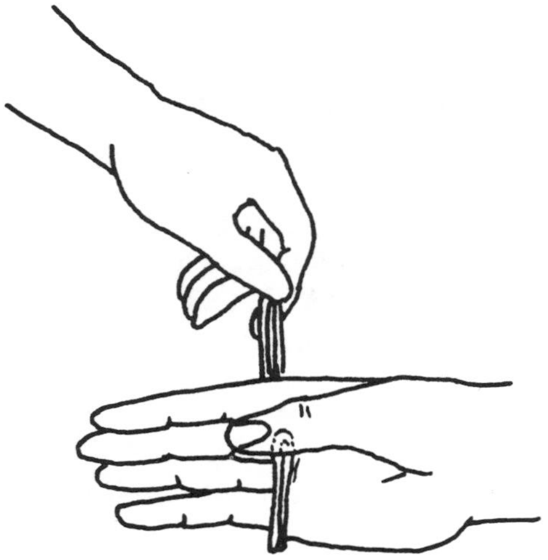

FIG. 2A 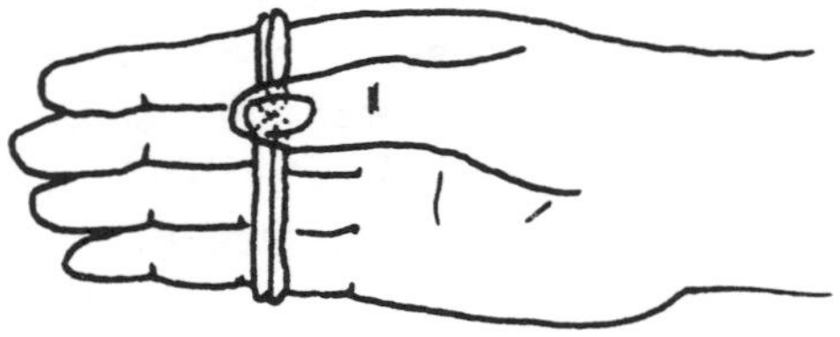   FIG. 2B

Next slip your left first and second fingers through the band, and pull the band to your left. Your right first and second fingers pull to the right. (Be sure to keep hold of the two ends of the rubber band underneath your right thumb), (FIG. 3).

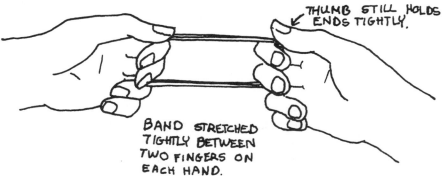

THUMB STILL HOLDS
ENDS TIGHTLY.

BAND STRETCHED
TIGHTLY BETWEEN
TWO FINGERS ON
EACH HAND.

FIG. 3

The above moves take only a second to perform. By the time the spectator is looking back up at you and giving you the time, you should be in position to perform phase two of the trick, THE BREAK: Stretch the band a few times be-tween your fingers, and on the third stretch LET GO OF THE LEFT END OF THE BAND (from underneath your right thumb), ALLOWING IT TO SHOOT ACROSS INTO YOUR LEFT HAND AND SLIDE BETWEEN YOUR LEFT THUMB AND FIRST FINGER (FIG. 4).

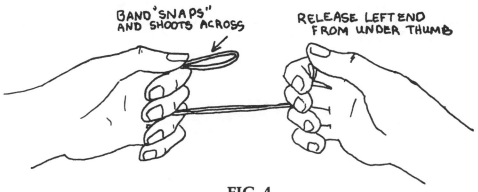

BAND "SNAPS" AND SHOOTS ACROSS

RELEASE LEFT END FROM UNDER THUMB

FIG. 4

Not only can an audible snapping sound be heard as you let go of the left end of the rubber band, but the spectator can actually see the band "break" and shoot across to the other hand, just as it would if the band really broke. The illusion is perfect!

If, after the band shoots across, there is a loop of rubber band sticking out from under your left thumb (FIG. 5), quickly cover the piece with your thumb (FIG. 6).

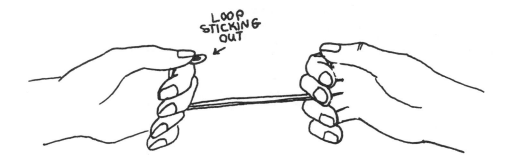

LOOP STICKING OUT

FIG. 5

(Occasionally, when I perform this trick, the spectator will be so convinced the band broke, she will turn away to get a new one. Since I want her to keep her attention focused on the rubber band I'm working with, I'll say, "Wait, watch..." and then I'll quickly restore the band as follows.

THE RESTORATION: To restore the "broken" rubber band, close your left hand around the band and blow on it. Then slowly open your hand and show the spectator that the band is completely restored. Extend your hand so the spectator can pick up the band and examine it (FIG. 7).

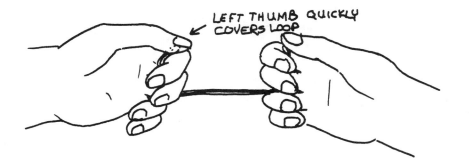

FIG. 6

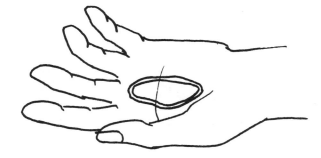

FIG. 7

FINAL COMMENT: Remember to keep the band stretched tight throughout the routine; otherwise there's a chance the band(s) will separate and the secret will be exposed.

TRICK #17

THE MYSTERIOUS MATCH

*To achieve any goal you must have
a burning desire."*

COMMENTS: This trick, like the previous one, THE CHEAP RUBBER BAND, is a great impromptu trick. It's quick, easy to do, and hits em' right between the eyes.

DESCRIPTION OF TRICK: Picking up a book of matches from the table, the performer opens it and asks the spectator to point to any match. After lighting the selected match, he places the matchbook onto the spectator's palm-up hand. He then extinguishes the lit match, and proceeds to cause it to disappear right before the spectator's eyes. Upon opening the matchbook, the spectator finds his selected BURNT match firmly affixed to the inside!

THE SECRET: Unbeknownst to the spectator, there is a burnt match already inside the book of matches when you start the trick. The way you cause his selected match to "disappear" is to literally throw it over your shoulder as you shake the match to extinguish it.

MATERIALS: A book of matches.

SET UP: Let's assume you're at a restaurant having lunch. When no one is looking, grab a book of matches off the table at which you are sitting, and excuse yourself to go to the rest room. Once there, bend back one of the matches in the center of the book.

Next, tear out one of the other matches and use it to light the match you just bent back. Let it burn for a few moments and then blow out both matches. Throw the torn-out match away, fold the bent burnt match back into the book, and close the cover (FIG. 1).

FIG. 1

When you return to the table, sneak the matchbook onto the table. (You can just pull the matches out of your pocket and start the trick, but doing it this way makes the trick appear more spontaneous.)

TO PERFORM: Ask the spectator if he would like to see something very weird. When he says, "yes" (who wouldn't?), say, "Hand me those matches on the table please." Take the matches from him, open them, and as you do so fold the burnt match BACK, and then place your thumb over it (FIG. 2).

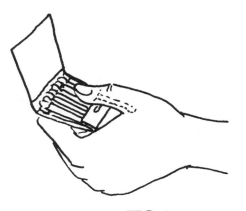

FIG. 2

For misdirection, as you're opening the book say, "Trust me, this is REALLY weird!" When he looks you in the eye as you say REALLY weird, that's when you bend back the match and put your thumb over it.

Next say, "Point to a match, any match." As you say this line, point to the matches in the center as if to demonstrate the area from which you want him to choose. If you do this, he will be more likely to select a match near the center, which is what you want. If he points to a match near one of the sides, the trick will still work, but it's not quite as strong.

Okay, tear out the match he points to, and start to close the match cover. As you do this, secretly bend the burnt match back into place (FIG. 3)

Have the spectator hold out his hand. Light the match you tore out and place the matchbook onto his hand.

You're now going to make the selected match vanish: Start to shake the match 3 or 4 times to extinguish it. On the fourth shake, let the match slip out from

between your thumb and first finger and fly over your shoulder out of sight (BE
SURE THE MATCH IS OUT BEFORE YOU TOSS IT, OTHERWISE SOME-
THING REALLY WEIRD WILL HAPPEN! (FIG. 4).

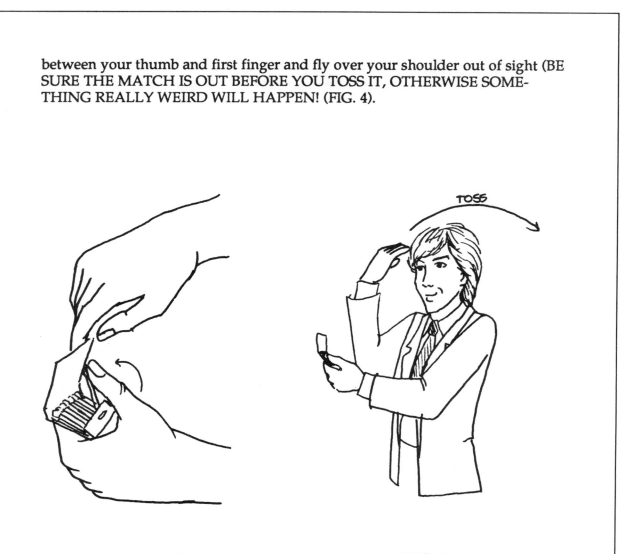

FIG. 3   FIG. 4

Continue to shake your hand as if you still had the match in it a few more times,
and then bring your hand down over the spectator's, and say, "Watch the match
slowly disappear right before your eyes." As you say, "...right before your
eyes," turn your hand over and show it to be empty. If it is done correctly, the
spectator will swear the match disappeared right then!

To end the trick, ask the spectator if he knows where the match is? When he
replies, "No," tell him to look inside the match book. As he sees the match
inside the book (FIG. 5), say, "Look it's fastened right to the match book." Then
say, "pretty weird, huh?"

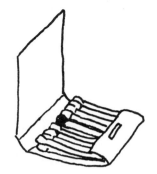

FIG. 5

FINAL COMMENT: IF you really want to blow em' away, perform the trick within a minute or two of setting up the burnt match. That way when the spectator opens the matches and discovers his match back in place, it will still be warm! This is a great convincer that it's the same match you tore out and lit moments before.

TRICK #18

THE VANISHING SALT SHAKER

Sign in a Milwaukee restaurant: "Come in and eat before we both starve."

COMMENTS: This is an excellent trick to do when you're at a restaurant with your client and the two of you are waiting for the waitress to bring your food.

DESCRIPTION OF TRICK: The performer offers to show the spectator a magic trick with a penny, a salt shaker and a napkin. After wrapping the salt shaker in the napkin, the performer covers the penny with the wrapped-up shaker. He states that when he lifts the shaker, the penny will be gone. However when the performer lifts the shaker the penny is still there. The performer offers to try the trick one more time. Suddenly, the performer brings his hand down smashing the napkin flat against the table — instead of the penny vanishing, the salt shaker has vanished!

THE SECRET: The salt shaker is secretly dropped into the performer's lap while the spectator is looking at the coin. However, the performer continues to act as if the salt shaker is still under the napkin until he is ready to make it vanish.

MATERIALS: A salt shaker, a paper napkin, and a penny.

TO PERFORM: Ask the spectator if he would like to see you make a coin disappear right before his eyes. Assuming he says yes, tightly wrap the napkin around the salt shaker so that, if you were to lift off the napkin, it would still retain the shape of the shaker (FIG. 1).

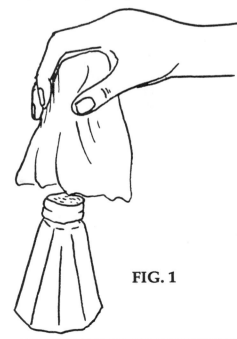

FIG. 1

Tell him that the reason for wrapping the shaker in the napkin is to protect the secret to the trick (which is true!). Next place the coin in the middle of the table. Tell him to keep his eyes glued to the spot on the table where the coin is. Now cover the coin with the wrapped-up shaker as you ask him if he would be amazed if, when you lifted up the shaker, the coin was gone? Again he should reply, "yes." Now stare at the spot where the coin is (you can't actually stare at the coin since it's under the shaker!) as you count "one, two, three!" When you count "three," a couple of things happen at once. First you lift the shaker with your right hand and bring it straight back to the edge of the table, then you point to the coin with your left hand as you say, "See, it's gone...and it has been re-placed with an exact duplicate coin!" As you say this tongue-in-check line, your right hand relaxes its grip on the salt shaker allowing it to fall into your lap (FIG. 2).

FIG. 2

If you say this line while pointing at the coin, the spectator will not notice the shaker falling into your lap, because all his attention is on the coin; since that is what he is expecting to see vanish.

Be sure to keep the edge of the napkin on the table so he doesn't accidentally catch a glimpse of the shaker falling from the napkin to your lap. Also, be sure to keep your legs close together; otherwise the sound of the shaker hitting your chair and then falling to the floor will alert the spectator to the fact that something is definitely not right!

The next step is to say, "Okay, I admit it, the trick didn't work, but let me try it one more time." Now place the napkin shell over the penny, being careful not to crush it prematurely. Then count to three, and on three bring your right hand down onto the napkin, squashing it like a pancake (FIG. 3).

FIG. 3

This should really catch the spectator off guard and you will completely fool him. Now simply crumple the napkin into a ball and say, "I never could get that darn coin to disappear anyway!"

At this point you can either leave the salt shaker in your lap and keep the spectator wondering, or you can reach under the table and bring out the salt shaker saying, "Well, here's an extra shaker we can use for lunch." The choice is up to you.

TRICK #19

X MARKS THE SPOT

"Be patient. You get the chicken by hatching the egg — not by smashing it open."

DESCRIPTION OF TRICK: The performer asks the spectator to extend both her hands, palm down, and then to close each hand into a tight fist. The performer then reaches over to an ashtray, removes a few of the ashes, and uses them to draw an X on top of the spectator's right fist. Next the performer says that he will try an experiment of telekinesis, the ability to move objects with the mind.

After concentrating on the X for a few seconds, the performer slowly rubs the X until the ashes disappear. The performer then asks the spectator if she knows where the X went to? When the spectator replies that she has no idea, the performer instructs her to slowly turn her LEFT hand over and open it up. Upon opening her left fist, the spectator is shocked to see that a black X has mysteriously appeared on the palm of her hand!

COMMENTS: This is a great trick to perform when you're at a restaurant or bar. The fact that it can be done without any special props makes this impromptu effect a real stunner.

THE SECRET: Unbeknownst to the spectator, you secretly made an X on the palm of her left hand before the trick even began.

MATERIALS: An ashtray with ashes in it.

SET UP: When no one is looking, dip your right first finger into the ashtray and get a smudge of ashes on your finger tip.

TO PERFORM: Ask the spectator if she would like to see something truly amazing. When she says yes, tell her to extend her hands toward you, palm down. As if to assist her, reach out with your right hand and take her LEFT hand, as your left hand takes her RIGHT hand. Bring her palm-down hands within approximately six inches of each other. It is while you are "positioning" her hands next to each other that your right first finger presses up on her left palm and draws an X (FIG. 1).

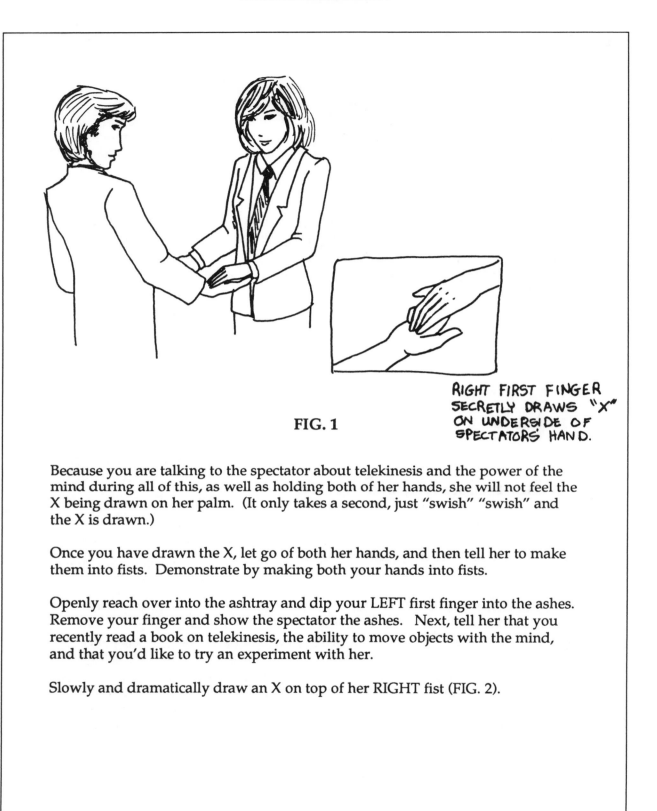

FIG. 1

RIGHT FIRST FINGER
SECRETLY DRAWS "X"
ON UNDERSIDE OF
SPECTATORS HAND.

Because you are talking to the spectator about telekinesis and the power of the mind during all of this, as well as holding both of her hands, she will not feel the X being drawn on her palm. (It only takes a second, just "swish" "swish" and the X is drawn.)

Once you have drawn the X, let go of both her hands, and then tell her to make them into fists. Demonstrate by making both your hands into fists.

Openly reach over into the ashtray and dip your LEFT first finger into the ashes. Remove your finger and show the spectator the ashes. Next, tell her that you recently read a book on telekinesis, the ability to move objects with the mind, and that you'd like to try an experiment with her.

Slowly and dramatically draw an X on top of her RIGHT fist (FIG. 2).

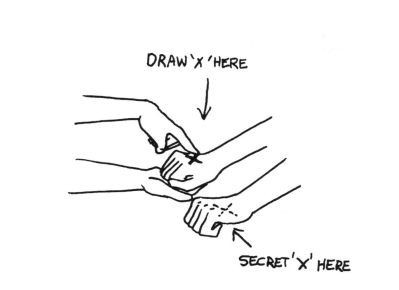

DRAW 'X' HERE

SECRET 'X' HERE

FIG. 2

Really make a big deal of the drawing of the X, as if the success of the experiment depends on the X being drawn just right. Pretend to concentrate really hard for a few seconds, and then using your RIGHT fingers, slowly rub the X until the ashes disappear. (The reason you use your right fingers to rub in the ashes is to cover up any ashes that may have been left on your finger from when you were setting up the person.)

Pretend like you're concentrating really hard and then ask the spectator if she knows where you made the X materialize? When she says no, say, "Open your left fist!" Watch the look on her face as she sees the black X on the palm of her hand. Believe me, if you have never had this old bar stunt pulled on you before, you have no idea how eerie it can be.

FINAL COMMENTS: For maximum impact, this trick is best played in a somewhat serious tone. The first time it was performed on me was at a party many years ago. The guy who performed it went into this whole long talk about voodoo, and how when he was in the jungles of Africa a real witch doctor showed him this bizarre stunt, etc... And the whole time I was laughing to myself, "Yeah, right, voodoo, sure...," but I have to be honest and admit that when I opened my hand and saw the X, I wasn't laughing anymore. It really freaked me out! When I was finally told the secret to the trick, I remember hitting myself upside the head thinking, "Oh man, I've been had!" Try it on a friend and see for yourself.

TRICK #20

THE LIE DETECTOR CARD TRICK

*"Blessed are our enemies, for they tell
us the truth when our friends flatter us."*

COMMENTS: Even a person who doesn't like card tricks really gets a kick out of this one. The idea of using a person's tone of voice as a way to find their card is fascinating to most people.

DESCRIPTION OF TRICK: The performer states that more and more businesses are requiring their employees to submit to polygraph or "lie detector" test. He says, "I am an expert in this particular field, and I have discovered that all that fancy equipment isn't necessary to give a lie detector test. All that is needed is a deck of cards!"

To prove his point, the performer hands a deck of cards to a spectator, requesting that she give them a shuffle.

Next he has her select a card from the middle of the deck, remember it, and return it to the pack. She is asked to give the pack as many cuts as she wishes.

Next the performer starts dealing the cards FACE UP onto her outstretched hand, with the request that she say the word "NO" as each card is dealt. Even if she sees her card, she is still to say the word "NO." The performer says that he will listen carefully to the tone of her voice and will be able to detect when she is lying to him.

After dealing approximately half the deck, the performer deals one more card and as the spectator says, "No," the performer smiles and says, "LIAR!" The spectator smiles as the card staring her in the face is her selection!

THE SECRET: As the spectator concludes her shuffle, you secretly glimpse and remember the bottom card of the deck. This bottom card will go on top of the spectator's card as the cards are cut, and thus when you deal the cards face up and see this KEY card again, you know the card immediately following it is the selection.

The nice thing about this trick is that because the spectator thinks you are using her tone of voice to tell you the name of her card, she never even suspects you are using a KEY card.

MATERIALS: A deck of cards.

SET UP: None.

TO PERFORM: Hand the cards to the spectator to be shuffled. When you take the deck back, secretly tilt the pack so you get a glimpse of the bottom card. REMEMBER THIS BOTTOM CARD, THIS IS YOUR KEY CARD.

Next tell the spectator to reach inside the center of the deck, remove a card and remember the name of it. Next, cut the deck and have her return the card ON TOP of the cut-off portion of the deck. PLACE THE BOTTOM HALF OF THE DECK ON TOP OF THE SPECTATOR'S CARD, THUS COMPLETING THE CUT. What the spectator doesn't know is that you have just placed the key card directly above her card (FIG. 1).

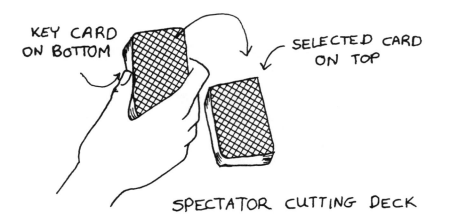

KEY CARD ON BOTTOM

SELECTED CARD ON TOP

SPECTATOR CUTTING DECK

FIG. 1

Have the spectator give the pack a few cuts, (This will not effect your ability to find her card). Now explain to her that you will use her voice to find the selected card. Tell her to say the word "NO" each time you turn a card face up. Remind her that even when she sees her card, she should still say the word "NO." Explain that you will carefully listen to the tone of her "NO'S" and will be able to tell when she is lying.

Holding the deck face down, begin to deal the cards face up, one at a time, onto the spectator's outstretched hand. Keep dealing until you turn over the KEY card. THE NEXT CARD WILL BE THE SPECTATOR'S CHOSEN CARD. Deal it onto her hand, and then wait for her to say "NO." When she does, immediately look her in the eye, smile, and say, "LIAR!"

The spectator will usually smile back and nod in agreement, signifying that is indeed her card.

FINAL COMMENT: If you want to have a little fun, try this trick on your spouse or significant other, and then afterward tell her she should never lie to you because, as she can see for herself, you will know!

TRICK #21

THE RAPPORT CARD TRICK

"We cannot all play the same instrument,
but we can all be in the same key."

COMMENTS: If the customer feels you are on the same wavelength as he is, you stand a good chance of making the sale. This card trick illustrates the tremendous results that are possible when you and your client are in rapport.

DESCRIPTION OF TRICK: After talking about the importance of having rapport with the customer, the performer hands the spectator two decks of cards requesting that he select one and return the other to the performer. This done, the performer and the spectator each shuffle their respective decks. Next the performer instructs the spectator to go through his deck, remove any card, memorize it, and then place the card on top of his deck. The performer states that he will do likewise with his deck.

This done, both give their respective decks numerous cuts, thus making it virtually impossible for either one to know the other's card. Next the performer hands his deck to the spectator, requesting that he go through the deck and remove the card he thought of, and that he, the performer, will go through the spectator's deck and remove the card that he thought of. Both cards are placed side by side, face down on the table. When both cards are turned over, they are seen to be identical! Obviously the performer and the spectator were in rapport.

THE SECRET: The nice part about this trick is that ordinary cards are used, and the trick requires no set up. The reason you were able to select the same card as the spectator is because you knew at which card he looked. How? By using a "key" card (just like in the previous trick.)

How the key card helps reveal the identity of the spectator's card will become apparent as you read on.

MATERIALS: Two decks of cards.

TO PERFORM: Hand both decks to the spectator and ask him to select one. Retrieve the one he did not select and instruct him to shuffle his deck while you shuffle yours.

Now fan your deck out in front of you FACE UP with both hands, so that both you and the spectator can see the faces of the cards. Request the spectator to do the same with his deck. It is while both decks are fanned out face up that you memorize the name of the TOP FACE UP CARD OF THE SPECTATOR'S FAN (FIG. 1). This is your key card.

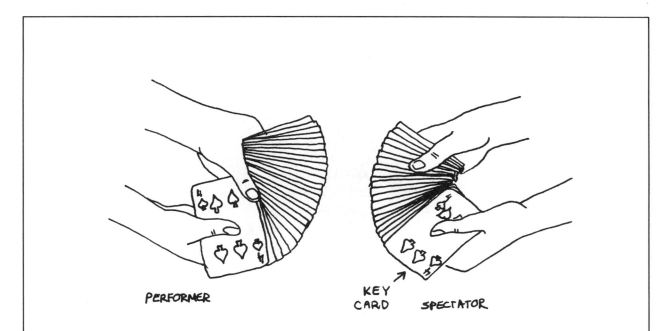

PERFORMER   KEY
                                             CARD   SPECTATOR

FIG. 1

You can tell the spectator that the reason for having the decks fanned out is so that when the two of you go to memorize one of the cards in the deck, you will each have a clear view of all the cards.

Note: if the spectator does not tilt his deck forward enough for you to see the faces of his cards, simply reach out with your hand and pull his deck down so you CAN see the faces. Do this under the pretext that you are looking to see if his deck contains any jokers. Your conversation would go something like this: "Now fan out your deck like this (fan out your deck)... oh I can't remember, did I take out the jokers from that deck?" (reach out and gently pull down his cards so you can see the faces, note the top card of the fan, the key card), and say, "Oh, I guess I did, fine..." and proceed with the trick. Just do it casually and he won't suspect a thing. Why should he? You haven't done anything yet.

Now tell the spectator to hold the deck in front of him so there is no way you can see any of his cards (you do the same with your deck). Now tell him to remove any one of the cards from his deck, memorize it, and then place it ON TOP of the deck (FIG. 2).

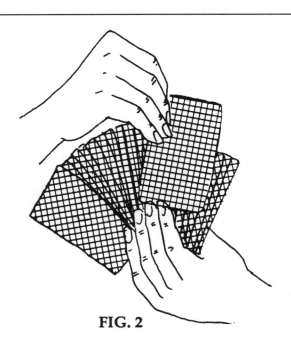

FIG. 2

Tell him you will do the same thing with your deck. Simply remove any card from the middle of your deck and place it on top of the deck. The card you select is unimportant and there is no need for you to memorize it.

Now tell the spectator to square up his deck, place it on the table and give it a couple of cuts (you do the same with your deck). The purpose for having the spectator cut the deck in this manner is twofold. First, it lets him think that he's mixing the cards up and thus making it impossible for you to know the location of the selected card, and secondly, it brings the key card DIRECTLY ON TOP OF THE CARD HE SELECTED (FIG. 3).

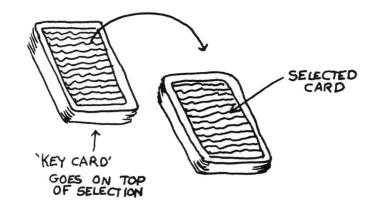

SELECTED CARD

'KEY CARD'
GOES ON TOP
OF SELECTION

FIG. 3

*He may cut the cards as many times as he wishes, as it will not effect the outcome of the trick. While he's cutting his deck, you should give your deck a couple of cuts too. When he's done cutting the cards, have him square up his deck (square up your deck as well). Next hand your deck to the spectator and ask him to remove the card he thought of and place it face down on the table, and tell him you will take his deck and remove the card you thought of and place it on the table.

Take his deck from him, fan it out with the faces toward you, and look for your key card. The card to the RIGHT of the key card will be the card the spectator selected. (FIG. 4).

FIG. 4

Remove this card and lay it face down on the table next to the card the spectator laid on the table. Now say, "On the count of three, you turn over the card you thought of and I'll turn over the card I thought of." By now the spectator will have a good idea of what's about to happen and will begin to say things like, "No way..."

On three turn your card over as the spectator turns his card over and watch the expression on his face as he sees that you thought of the exact same card as he did!

FINAL COMMENTS: This trick is a real miracle when performed correctly. While it isn't very difficult to perform, it must be rehearsed so that your presentation of the trick is first class.

Also, notice how you refer to his card as the one "you merely thought of." The reason for this is so that later on when he tells his friends about the card trick, he will say, "He just thought of a card and I just thought of a card, and they matched!" And he will subconsciously leave out the part about removing the card from the deck and placing it on top, etc.

This is a great trick, don't pass it up!

* While there is a small chance of the spectator cutting between the key card and the one he selected, it really makes no difference. This is because if you fan the deck and see that the bottom card of the deck is the key card then you know that the top card, the card that would have been to the right, is the spectator's card!

TRICK #22

THE STUCK-UP BUSINESS CARD

*"Business is a lot like tennis — those
who don't serve well end up losing."*

COMMENTS: This offbeat trick is admittedly a little bizarre; however the person for whom you perform the trick is likely to hold onto the business card with the "funny orange stickers" on it for a long time.

DESCRIPTION OF TRICK: The performer removes from his pocket a packet of rubber-banded business cards, a pen, and a 3/4 inch round orange sticker. He asks the spectator to sign his first name on the sticker. The performer then has the spectator peel off the signed sticker and stick it onto the FRONT of one of the performer's business cards. The performer then turns the business card face down and sets it in front of the spectator.

Next the performer states that he will duplicate the spectator's actions, except that since there are no more stickers left, he will have to use his imagination and pretend! Suiting actions to words, the performer pretends to write his first name on an invisible sticker, mimes peeling it off, and then pretends to place the sticker onto the business card.

The performer then asks the spectator if he can SEE the performer's signed sticker on the business card. The spectator, who is beginning to wonder whether the performer is playing with a full deck, says "no." To which the performer replies, "It's there, you just have to know where to look." The performer tells the spectator to turn over the business card. When the spectator does this, he is amazed to see that right next to his signed sticker is another orange sticker, with the performer's signature on it!

THE SECRET: A special half-business card, which is used to conceal the performer's signed orange sticker from the spectator, makes this effect possible.

MATERIALS: A stack of your business cards, a sheet of 3/4 inch round orange stickers (or any other color), a rubber band, scissors, and a pen.

TO CONSTRUCT: Use the scissors to cut one of your business cards in half (FIG. 1).

FIG. 1

Now take one of the orange stickers and write your first name on it, then peel it off and stick it on the RIGHT side of one of your business cards (FIG. 2).

Take this business card with the sticker on it, and place it on top of the stack of business cards. Now place the right side of the business card you cut in half on TOP of the business card with the orange sticker (so the orange sticker is covered). Now place the rubber band around the stack of cards so that it covers the seam where the half card and the card beneath it meet (FIG. 3).

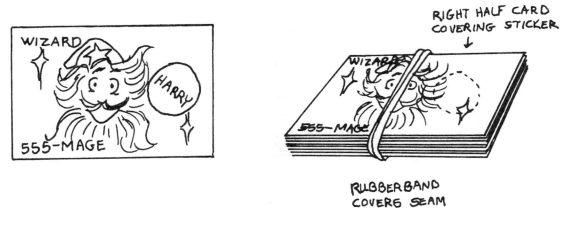

FIG. 2   FIG. 3

The half-card, along with the strategically placed rubber band create the illusion that the top card of the stack is completely normal!

Finally, use the scissors to cut off one orange sticker from the sheet of stickers.

SET UP: Place the lone orange sticker, along with the rubber banded stack of cards and the pen into your coat pocket, and you're ready to go.

TO PERFORM: Take out the rubber-banded cards, the pen, and the sticker, and lay them on the table in front of you. Hand the pen to the spectator and have him "autograph" the orange sticker. Then tell him to remove the sticker from the wax paper to which it is presently stuck.

As he is doing this, pick up your business cards and hold them in your right hand, with your thumb on the half-card. Now have the spectator place his signed sticker onto the LEFT side of the top business card (your right thumb is there to prevent the half-card from accidentally falling off). While the spectator believes his sticker is going on the top card, it is actually going on the second card of the stack, the one with YOUR orange sticker on it (FIG. 4).

FIG. 4

You're now going to remove this "double stickered" business card from the stack. However, if you were to just pull the card straight out, YOUR hidden orange sticker would be exposed. Since you don't want this to happen, grasp hold of the end of the card with your left thumb and first finger, and TURN THE CARD FACE DOWN AS YOU REMOVE IT FROM UNDERNEATH THE RUBBER BAND (FIG. 5).

FIG. 5

Place the card face down in front of the spectator.

The trick is really over now as far as you're concerned, as you've completed all the "dirty work." You are ahead of the spectator without his knowing it. Yet as far as he is concerned, nothing has really happened so far. All you've done is had him sign his name on a sticker, and then placed that sticker onto a business card which you then set face down in front of him.

To bring the trick to its climax, tell the spectator that you too will sign a sticker; however since you don't have any more left, you will have to pretend! Go through the motions of signing a sticker and then blowing on it as if to help the ink dry. Then mime pulling the sticker off the wax paper, carrying it over to the face-down business card, and then dropping the sticker onto the card. Ask the spectator if he can see your signed sticker. Regardless of his answer, have him turn the card over. Watch the look on his face as he sees the sticker with your name on it right next to his signed sticker!

PART VI

TRADE SHOW AND PRODUCT TIE-IN TRICKS

The tricks in this section are designed to be performed at trade shows or any other event where you want to use magic to help sell your product. Some of the routines I've included are word-for-word, just as I performed them. This is so you can see the thinking that goes into putting together a trade show or "product pitch" routine.

As you read each trick, you should be thinking of ways to apply the magic to your own product. In fact, it's a good idea to put on your CREATIVITY HAT while you're reading through the tricks.

With your CREATIVITY HAT on, think to yourself at every turn of the page, "How can I make this trick fit MY product?" "What changes will need to be made if I decide to use this one?" "Wait till my boss sees this!"

Creating new ideas is not only fun but can actually lead to practical, money-making ways to increase your income.

TRICK #23

THE 3 MAGIC ROPES

"Anything you buy at a low price that you don't need is not a bargain."

COMMENTS: I've decided to open this section on trade show magic with a trick I call "The 3 Magic Ropes," because it really illustrates how effectively magic can be used to sell a product or service. In fact, with a little imagination, you can take this trick and tie it into ANY product or service.

While the basic effect of the trick is that of taking three different lengths of rope and stretching them so they all become the same length, the real trick is to hammer home the benefits of your product to your audience. In the following example, I will use a fictitious computer company called "Pineapple Computers" to demonstrate how to tie in a product with the "3 Magic Ropes" trick.

DESCRIPTION OF TRICK: Holding up three pieces of rope, each a different length, the performer says to his audience, "Not all computer companies are the same. Many have one or two outstanding features, but tend to fall short in other areas. For instance, this short piece of rope represents customer service. As the length of the rope suggests, many computer companies tend to come up short when it comes to good customer service."

"Or take this medium piece of rope, which represents a product's quality. While all companies claim their products are top quality, I think you'll agree that there is a vast difference in the levels of quality available when it comes to computers.

"And finally, the third piece of rope, the longest one, represents a company's reputation. Many companies are long on stories as to how reputable they are, but the truth is that many are simply out to make a buck.

"Friends, while many companies may talk about customer service, quality and reputation, we at Pineapple Computers believe in giving our customers 100% customer service, 100% quality for their dollars, backed by our reputation which is 100% honest!" (As this is said the performer magically stretches all 3 ropes into the same length!)

He then proceeds to count the ropes one at a time from one hand into the other as he says: "That's right, at Pineapple Computers, we feel that serving our customer, having a top quality product, and the best reputation in the business, all make for a winning combination!"

"Thus, when deciding to purchase a computer, watch out for companies who claim to have good customer service, top quality, and an outstanding reputation, but in reality do not." (As the performer says this last line, he changes the 3 ropes back into their original lengths of short, medium, and long.) To conclude the routine, he hands the ropes out for examination as he says, "So why take chances? Go with the company that has it all, go with Pineapple computers!"

SECRET: The illusion of making the three ropes appear to be the same length is created by cleverly switching the ends of two of the ropes. This "switching of the ends" enables you to loop the short rope around the long rope so that when you "stretch" the ropes they appear to all be the same length. The illusion is further enhanced by the use of a "false count," which makes it appear as if you're showing all three ropes separately, when in fact you are not.

MATERIALS: 3 pieces of 1/2 inch rope or cord. Thick shiny cord, either red or blue, which can be purchased at any fabric store in the curtain accessories section, works best.

TO CONSTRUCT: Here are the lengths of the 3 pieces of rope needed to perform the trick: The short piece should be approximately 12 inches in length. The medium piece of rope should be approximately 30 inches in length, and the long piece should be approximately 48 inches long (FIG. 1). It is a good idea to wrap clear tape around the ends of the cord or rope. This is to prevent them from fraying or unraveling.

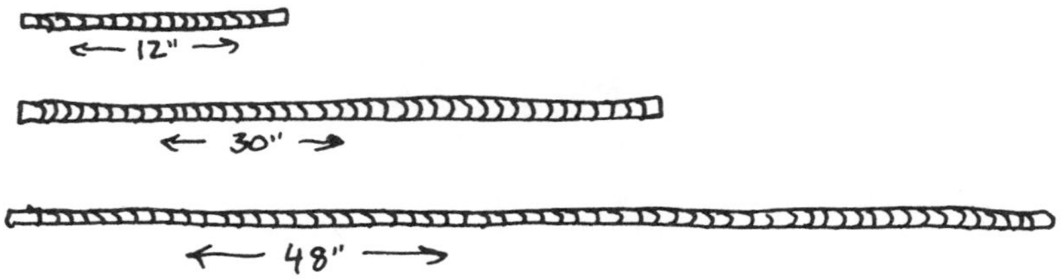

←— 12" —→

←— 30" —→

←— 48" —→

FIG. 1

TO PERFORM: (I suggest you go through this routine with the ropes in hand, as just reading through sans rope can be confusing.) I will continue to use Pineapple computers in my example; however you, of course, would fill in the name of your company or product.

Hold up the three pieces of rope (short, medium, and long — from left to right) in your left hand, clipping them underneath your left thumb. After talking about how all computer companies are not the same, take the SHORT piece of rope with your right hand and hold it up for the audience to see. As you do this say, "This piece of rope represents customer service which, as you can see by the size of the rope, is a department in which many companies tend to come up short." Place the short piece of rope back into your left hand, into its original position closest to your thumb.

Next your right hand holds up the MEDIUM rope as you say, "This medium length of rope represents a product's quality, which I think you'll agree varies greatly from one computer company to another. Replace the medium rope back into your left hand into the middle position, and then take hold of the LONG rope. Hold up the LONG rope as you say, "And finally, the third piece of rope, the longest one, which represents a company's reputation. Many companies are long on stories as to how reputable they are, but the truth is that many are out simply to make a buck.

Place the long rope back into the left hand, so the ropes are back in there original order, from left to right: short, medium, and long (FIG. 2).

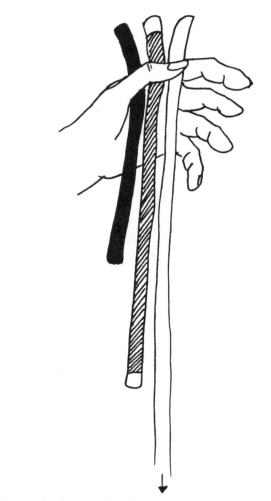

FIG. 2

Next you are going to bring up the three ends of the ropes that are hanging down, and place them next to the other three ends which are already under your left thumb. Do this one end at a time, starting with the SHORT PIECE of rope.

However, when you bring up the end of the short piece, YOU ARE GOING TO
SWITCH IT FOR THE END OF THE LONG PIECE, which is already under your
thumb (FIGS. 3A & 3B).

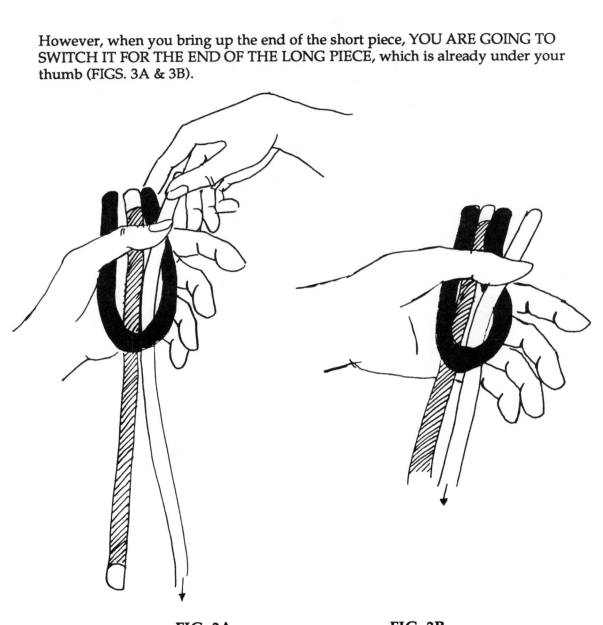

FIG. 3A   **FIG. 3B**

Don't make a big deal out of this. Just casually switch the two ends.
Remember, the audience has no idea what you're doing at this point. It should
just look like you're bringing up the end of the short rope, placing it along side
the long rope,and then adjusting them so the ends are even. That's all.
Next bring up the other two ends, BUT DO NOT SWITCH THEM! Simply bring
up the medium end, and then the long end. All six ends are now held in
position under your left thumb (FIG. 4).

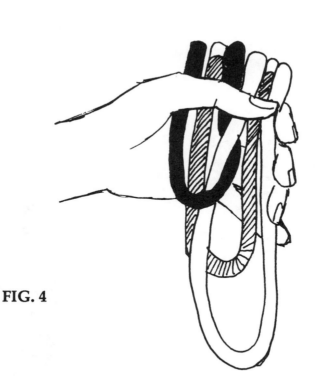

FIG. 4

As you're bringing up each of the ends, the patter that corresponds with the moves is as follows: As you're bringing up the short end (and performing the switch) say, "Friends, while many companies may talk about customer service..." (Now bring up the medium end) "quality"... (Now bring up the long end) "and reputation..." (As you say "reputation," you are bringing up the third and final end. So now all three ends are underneath your left thumb, which is now holding all six ends in place).

Continuing, you say, "We at Pineapple Computers believe in giving our customers 100% customer service, 100% quality for their dollars, backed by our reputation which is 100% honest!" It is as you say, "...backed by our reputation which is 100% honest!" that you stretch the ropes so they all become the same length. Here's how: First grab all six ends of the ropes and pull them up approximately one or two inches, so the secret loop goes up into your left palm. THIS IS IMPORTANT! If you forget this "pulling up of the ropes" just before stretching, then when you do go to stretch the ropes, the audience will see the loop (where the short and long rope connect), and you'll expose the secret!

Okay, so you've pulled the secret loop up into your left hand, great. Next your right hand takes hold of the three ends of the rope on the RIGHT, and slowly pulls them to the right as your left hand holds on to its three ends, along with the secret loop (FIG. 5).

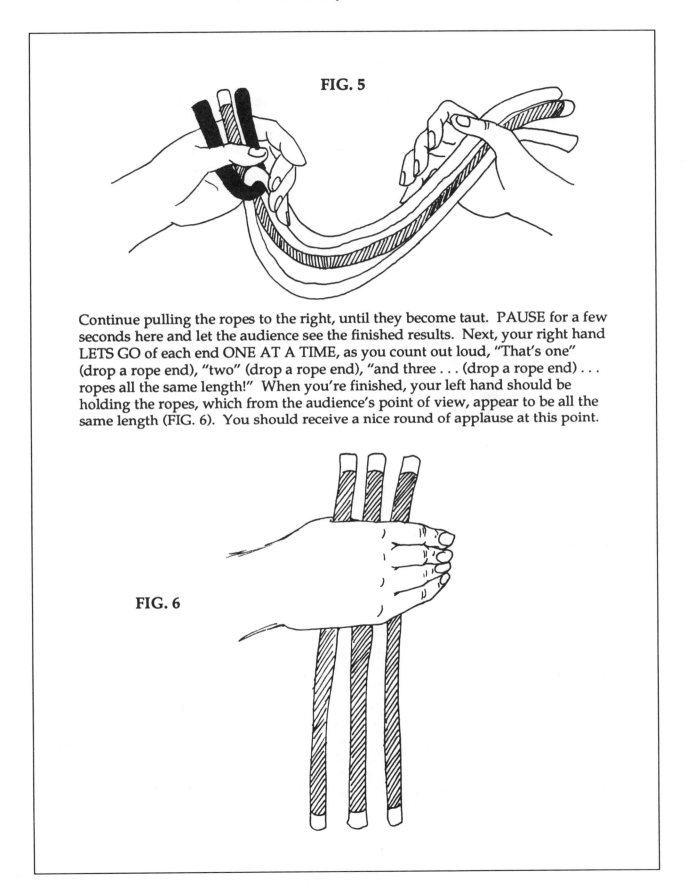

FIG. 5

Continue pulling the ropes to the right, until they become taut. PAUSE for a few seconds here and let the audience see the finished results. Next, your right hand LETS GO of each end ONE AT A TIME, as you count out loud, "That's one" (drop a rope end), "two" (drop a rope end), "and three . . . (drop a rope end) . . . ropes all the same length!" When you're finished, your left hand should be holding the ropes, which from the audience's point of view, appear to be all the same length (FIG. 6). You should receive a nice round of applause at this point.

FIG. 6

Now you are going to perform the false count. The purpose of the count is to further embellish the illusion of the ropes being separate and of equal lengths.

After you have "stretched" the ropes, and let go of the ends, your right hand takes hold of the CENTER rope (the medium rope), BETWEEN YOUR THUMB AND FIRST FINGER (more specifically, the rope goes deep into the "crotch" of the right thumb). The right hand then pulls the medium rope to the right until it clears the other two (FIG. 7). As you pull the rope to the right, let it slide through your fingers before falling away (rather than just dropping an end — it looks smoother this way).

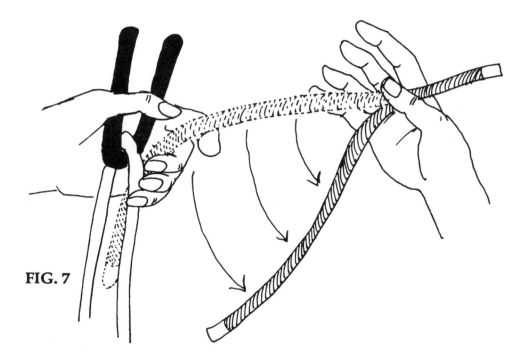

FIG. 7

Next you're going to apparently take a second rope from the left hand. However what you actually do is SWITCH THE SINGLE PIECE OF ROPE in your right hand FOR THE TWO ROPES IN YOUR LEFT HAND. Here's how: Bring the hands together, the right hand clipping its single rope in the crotch of the right thumb, and the left hand holding the two ropes in the crotch of the left thumb. The first and second fingers of both hands are opened like scissors. As the two hands touch, the right hand passes in front of the left, and the right first and second finger clamp down on the two pieces of rope in the left hand. AT THE SAME TIME the first and second fingers of the left hand clamp down on the single piece of rope in the right hand (FIG. 8).

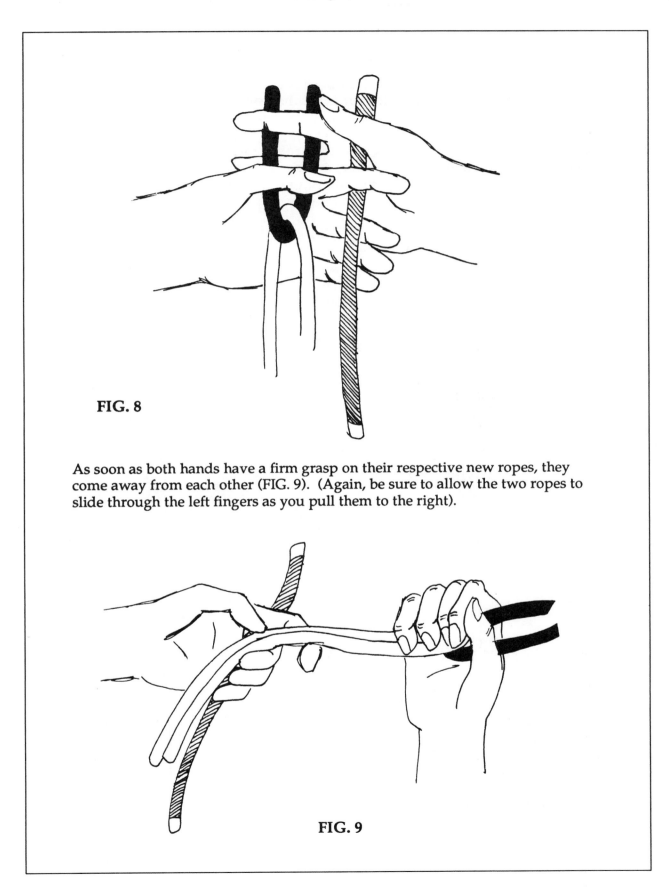

FIG. 8

As soon as both hands have a firm grasp on their respective new ropes, they come away from each other (FIG. 9). (Again, be sure to allow the two ropes to slide through the left fingers as you pull them to the right).

FIG. 9

Finally, the left hand, which is now holding a single piece of rope (the medium length piece, which was originally counted as the first rope), holds the rope up for the audience to see; the audience believes they are now being shown the third and final rope.

This switch does take practice in front of a mirror to get down smoothly, but once you get it down, it looks like you are simply counting three separate ropes from one hand into the other.

The lines that go with the false count are as follows: As you count the first rope say, "That's right, at Pineapple Computers, we feel that serving our customers..." (now perform switch, showing second rope) "Having a top quality product...." (now hold up third rope in left hand) "and the best reputation in the business make for a winning combination!"

Place the two pieces of rope in your right hand back into your left hand, UNDERNEATH YOUR LEFT THUMB and TO THE LEFT of the single piece already in your left hand. You can use your pinkie to keep the medium rope from falling out as you do this. (FIG. 10).

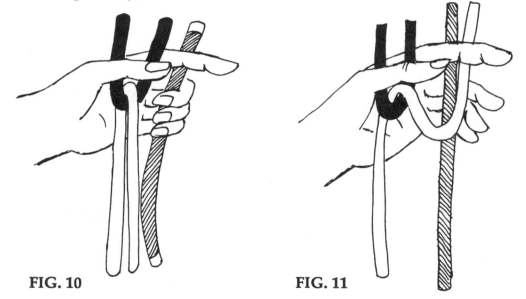

FIG. 10   FIG. 11

Next you are going to magically restore the ropes to their original lengths. Here's how: With your right hand reach down and grab one of the ends of the long piece of rope, (It doesn't matter which end you grab, as long as you DON'T GRAB THE END OF THE MEDIUM PIECE OF ROPE). Bring this end up and place it between your left first and second fingers (FIG. 11).

Now take hold of the three ends of rope FARTHEST TO THE RIGHT, with your right hand. HOLD ON TIGHTLY to these three ends as you give the rope a hard shake, while simultaneously LETTING GO OF EVERYTHING IN YOUR LEFT HAND. If you have done everything correctly, you should be left holding three pieces of rope in your right hand; a short, a medium, and a long.

As you perform this last move, you say "So why take chances? Go with the company that has it all, go with Pineapple computers!" You can now hand the ropes out for examination.

When this trick is performed smoothly, it never fails to hold an audience's attention. However you must practice the trick to the point that the moves with the rope become second nature, so that you are free to concentrate on selling your product.

Remember, literally any product or service can be tied into this trick. All you really need to come up with are 3 points or benefits that you wish to make, and then simply talk about them as you do the trick. For instance, if you sell cars, you could talk about how your company designs its products with SAFETY, PERFORMANCE, AND FUEL ECONOMY as its primary goals. And while some companies may emphasize one area over another, "Putt-Putt Incorporated," your company, focuses on all three areas when designing their cars.

As you can see, when it comes to coming up with ideas for product and service tie-ins, the sky's the limit.

TRICK #24

THE CROCKER BANK BROCHURES TRICK

*"A bank is a place where you can keep the
government's money until the IRS asks for it."*

COMMENTS: This routine came about when Crocker Bank hired me to do a magic show at a dinner for their top executives. I wanted to incorporate some of their products into my show, as I knew this would greatly increase the chances of my being asked back to future Crocker events. Walking into a local Crocker Bank Branch, I took a handful of their brochures home, whereupon I proceeded to come up with the following routine. I will use the Crocker brochures to describe the trick, but as you will readily see, any company's brochures can be used for this routine.

DESCRIPTION OF TRICK: The performer directs the audience's attention to a 2' x 3' white piece of cardboard, which is resting on an easel. Attached to the cardboard are five Crocker Bank brochures (FIG. 1).

FIG. 1

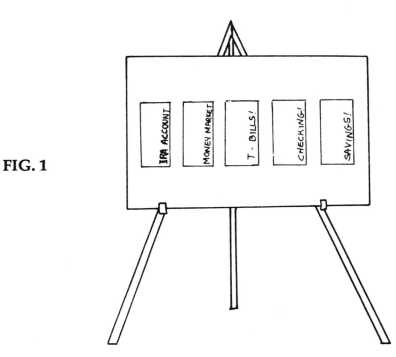

The Brochures are all different. One is about Crocker's Savings Account, one is about their Checking account, one is about their IRA account, one is about their Money Market Mutual Funds account, and one is about their T - bill account.

The performer says, "Ladies and Gentlemen, part of making a lot of money in life comes from knowing how to invest your money wisely." Picking up a large envelope from the table, he continues, "I have here inside this envelope a giant-sized one dollar bill." He removes the bill from the envelope. He then turns to the vice president of Crocker and says, "Mr. Shapiro, in a moment I'm going to ask you a question, but before I do, I want you to answer me honestly; have we prearranged anything whatsoever?" "No? Fair enough." Now Mr. Shapiro, you see before you five of your company's brochures, mounted on this piece of cardboard. All of them are excellent investments under the proper circumstances. I'd like you to tell me which one of these accounts you'd like to invest this dollar bill in right now. Please don't let me influence your decision, as you have your choice of any one of the five accounts."

Mr. Shapiro: "I'd put my money into the T- BILL account." "Very good Mr. Shapiro, then into the T- BILL account your dollar goes." The performer takes a piece of tape which has been resting on the side of the easel and uses it to tape the dollar directly over the T - BILL brochure.

Continuing, the performer says, "Ladies and Gentlemen, I have a little confession to make. Before anyone came into the room tonight, I made a prediction. What did I predict?   I predicted the brochure Mr. Shapiro would select. In fact, I made my choice even before Mr. Shapiro knew he would be asked to select a brochure. And yet as impossible as it may seem, my prediction was 100% correct!" And with that the performer tears off the T - BILL brochure from the board, and reveals a message. The message says: Mr. Shapiro will select the T - Bill Account!

The performer, sensing what the audience may be thinking, then proceeds to tear down the other four brochures. There is nothing written on them or on the board. The performer has correctly predicted which brochure the bank vice-president would pick! But how?

THE SECRET: The question you're probably asking yourself right now is, "What would have happened if he had selected a different brochure?" Answer: It would not have mattered. Regardless of which brochure Mr. Shapiro selected, I would have revealed a correct prediction. You got it, there were five predictions; one for each brochure! The real secret of the trick is keeping the 5 predictions hidden from the audience until you're ready to reveal the one that matches the spectator's selection.

MATERIALS: To perform this trick, you will need five brochures from your own company or from the company you'll be addressing. (I will continue using the Crocker Bank brochures throughout the explanation.)

Also needed is a large sturdy piece of white cardboard, 2' x 3', a roll of masking take, an 8" x 10" piece of white cardboard, a 10" x 13" manila envelope, 2 giant-sized one dollar bills (each measuring 5 1/4" x 12 1/4"), a piece of heavy white paper 10 1/2" x 24 1/2", a black felt tip marking pen, a pencil, some rubber cement, and an easel.

These giant-sized dollar bills can be found at most joke shops or stationery stores. (You could, of course, try making an enlargement of a real dollar bill on a copying machine. However I'm not sure how the U.S. Treasury Department would feel about this!)

TO CONSTRUCT: Take your two large-sized dollar bills, and glue one face up and the other face down on top of the 10 1/2" x 24 1/2" piece of paper. The bills top edges should be touching each other, so that one of the bills is upside down. The bills should completely cover the piece of paper. (FIG. 2).

FIG. 2

When the glue is dry, you can close up the dollar bill and show it on both sides. What the audience doesn't know is that one of your hidden predictions will be on the inside of the dollar, should you need to use it.

Next take the five brochures and tape them onto the large piece of cardboard, from left to right: 1) IRA, 2) MONEY MARKET MUTUAL FUNDS, 3) T - BILLS, 4) CHECKING, 5) SAVINGS. The best way to tape them in place is to take 2 pieces of masking tape approximately 2" long, and bend them back on themselves, so that you now have two 1" double sided pieces of tape. Now place one piece on the back of a brochure near the top, one on the back near the bottom, and then carefully adhere the brochure to the board. Do this with all 5 brochures. Be sure to leave the same amount of space between each brochure so your display looks nice.

Now carefully draw a line all the way around the outer edge of the of the center brochure, the T - BILLs brochure, using the pencil. Carefully remove the brochure, and using your felt tip marker, write inside the just-formed rectangle the following: Mr. Shapiro (obviously, you use whatever name is appropriate) will select the T - BILL account (FIG. 3).

FIG. 3

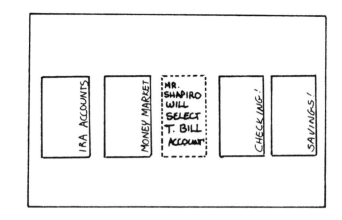

When the ink has dried, carefully replace the T - BIll brochure. You now have prediction # 1 hidden. To make secret prediction #2, turn the board over, and on the back side in large letters write: Mr. Shapiro will select the MONEY MARKET MUTUAL FUNDS account (FIG. 4).

MR. SHAPIRO WILL SELECT
THE
MONEY MARKET
            MUTUAL FUND   FIG. 4

To make secret prediction #3, take the 8 x 10 piece of white cardboard and write on it: Mr. Shapiro will select the CHECKING account. To make secret prediction #4, simply turn the card over, and on the back write: Mr. Shapiro will select the SAVINGS account. Place this card inside the envelope, with the CHECKING account side facing up, toward the natural seam of the envelope (FIG. 5).

FIG. 5

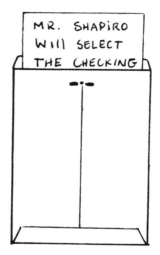

Next open up the gimmicked dollar bill, and on the inside write: Mr. Shapiro will select the IRA account. This is secret prediction #5 (FIG. 6).

MR. SHAPIRO WILL
SELECT THE IRA
ACCOUNT

FIG. 6

Close the dollar bill and place it inside the envelope, with the secret card.

SET UP: Place the board with the five brochures attached on the easel (FIG. 1). Place a small piece of masking tape on one of the legs of the easel and place the envelope on a table next to where you're performing and you're all set to go.

TO PERFORM: As you can see, the beauty of this trick is that all the work is done before you even walk up to perform the trick! All you need to do is wait until the spectator makes his choice and then reveal the matching prediction.

If he selects the IRA brochure, you pull it off the board (this is the reason you use masking tape, as it is less likely to tear the board and is reuseable) and reveal prediction #1. You then cancel out the thought that all of the brochures have something behind them by removing the other four brochures.

If he selects the MONEY MARKET brochure, you dramatically turn the board around and show prediction #2.

If he selects the CHECKING brochure, draw the audience's attention to the envelope from which you removed the dollar bill, and which has been in plain sight throughout the demonstration. Then hold the envelope so that the SEAM SIDE FACES THE AUDIENCE, thus assuring that when you remove the piece of cardboard, the side stating that Mr. Shapiro selected the CHECKING account will be showing.

Of course if he selects the SAVINGS brochure, then you simply turn the envelope around before removing the cardboard.

Finally, if the spectator selects the IRA brochure, you state that the dollar bill which you taped up over his selected brochure contains a prediction. You then open it up and show the audience prediction #5.

Remember, you tape the bill over whichever brochure he selects. If he picks any brochure other than the IRA one, you forget about the bill and draw the audience's attention to the matching prediction, whichever one that may be.

FINAL COMMENTS: Remember, it's very important that when you do reveal the correct prediction, you act as if it is the ONLY prediction you had. If the audience even slightly suspects that you had an "out" (an alternative prediction), the trick is ruined.

By the way, if you want to make the trick up so that you can use it over and over, simply write, "You will select..." rather than, "Mr. Shapiro will select..." for each of the predictions. While the trick is a little less personal this way, you have the advantage of being able to perform it over and over without having to make up a new set of predictions each time.

This trick has many, many possibilities as virtually any product or service can be tied in to this unique magical presentation.

TRICK #25

THE PREPCO DART BOARD ROUTINE

"Some resort ads don't always tell the truth. One place that promised 'miles of uncrowded beaches' turned out to be a naval gunnery range."

COMMENTS: When Prepco, a large food distribution company, hired me to perform at their company Christmas party, they gave me a great big box filled with all kinds of delicious samples of their products. Along with the yummy food samples was a stack of flyers, each having a picture of one of their food products on the front. After a bit of brainstorming, I came up with the following routine. (Once again, while I use pictures of food products in this routine, you can use pictures of ANY product including cars, computers, flowers, sporting goods, different kinds of liquors, etc.

DESCRIPTION OF TRICK: The performer draws the audience's attention to a large cardboard poster which is resting on an easel. Displayed on the poster are pictures of some 20 different kinds of food products the company sells. Next, the performer holds up an envelope which he states contains a prediction. He sets the envelope aside saying that he will come back to it.

The performer then hands a dart to the owner of the company, requesting that he throw the dart at the product-covered board. The owner throws the dart and it lands on (for example) the picture of the pretzels. The performer then opens up the prediction envelope and removes a piece of cardboard which he hands to a member of the audience. He asks the audience member to read aloud the food item the performer predicated the owner would select. The person reads aloud, "PRETZELS!"

THE SECRET: An extremely clever writing instrument is secretly used to indicate which food was selected through an opening in the back of the envelope.

MATERIALS: A large piece of cardboard 4' x 4' (the cardboard must have at least a 1/4" layer of foam between its layers — so the dart will have something to stick into when thrown. The cardboard is available at most art stores and is called mounting board.)

Also needed are an 8 1/2" x 11" manila envelope, an 8" x 10" piece of white cardboard, access to a typewriter, a band- style ring, a pencil WITH SOFT LEAD, clear tape, 20 pictures of food (or whatever products you choose to use), a can of spray-on glue, scissors, a dart and an easel.

TO CONSTRUCT: Coat one side of the 4' x 4' board with spray-on glue and carefully cover the treated side with your product pictures (FIG. 1).

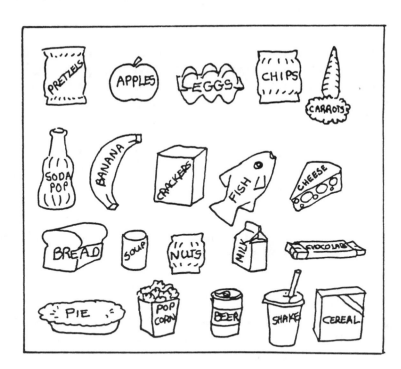

FIG. 1

Use the scissors to cut a 6" x 8" window in the back of the manila envelope (FIG. 2).

FIG. 2

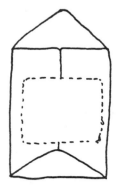

Take the piece of 8" x 10"cardboard, feed it into the typewriter, and approximately 4" from the top type out the sentence: I PREDICT MR. DRUCKER WILL SELECT: (Obviously you would type in the name of a V.I.P. at your presentation.) Directly underneath this, type out the names of your 20 products, in two neat rows, side by side. IMPORTANT: To the LEFT of each product's name, type a 1/2" line (FIG. 3).

___	BREAD	___	PIE
___	APPLE	___	SOUP
___	EGGS	___	NUTS
___	CHIPS	___	MILK
___	CARROT	___	HERSHEY
___	COKE	___	PRETZELS
___	BANANA	___	POPCORN
___	CRACKERS	___	BEER
___	FISH	___	SHAKE
___	CHEESE	___	CEREAL

FIG. 3

Place the typed list inside the envelope so you're able to see the list through the window — close the envelope using the clasp (FIG. 4).

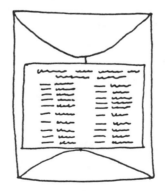

FIG. 4

Next, crack open the pencil, and break off a 1/2" piece of lead. Now securely tape this piece of lead to the left side of the ring, so it's pointing down (FIG. 5).

FIG. 5

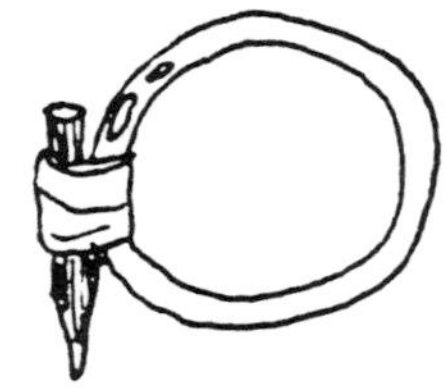

SET UP: Place the ring on your right third finger, the board on the easel, and the envelope, window side down, on a nearby table, along with the dart.

TO PERFORM: After showing the audience the board with all the products pictured on it, hold up the envelope (be careful not to expose the backside with the window). As you do this say, "Inside this envelope I have a prediction of which one of those twenty food items up on the board, I believe will be selected in just a few moments.

Hand the dart to the person you have selected to be "dart thrower" and instruct him to stand back approximately 10' from the board. Next say, "Now Mr. Drucker, you can either try to aim for a particular product or you can just throw caution to the winds and let the dart fall where it may... the choice is up to you. When I count to three, let 'er go. One, two, THREE!" When you say three, he will throw the dart at the board. If it sticks into a particular food item, that's great. If it lands between two items, give your thrower a choice of which item he thinks the dart is nearer. If the dart hits the board and then falls to the floor, simply pick it up and hand it back to the thrower, requesting that he try again. As you're handing him the dart, you can throw in this line: "You're going to have to throw just a little bit harder, Mr. Drucker, because as you know our products are TOUGH and made to last a lifetime." Obviously the line should be delivered with a friendly smile.

Okay, he has thrown the dart, and as in our example in DESCRIPTION OF TRICK, let's suppose he hit the picture of the bag of pretzels. Say, "Well, I think it's safe to say you selected the pretzels." Then walk over to the table and pick up the prediction envelope with your LEFT hand. Next say to the audience, "You would have to admit it would be pretty amazing if, inside this envelope, I had a prediction that said that Mr. Drucker would select the pretzels. Well I do... Heck, I think I can even smell the aroma of pretzels coming from the envelope!" It is as you deliver this last line that you place your right hand palm down on the back of the envelope, SO THAT THE PIECE OF LEAD IS RESTING RIGHT ON TOP OF THE LINE NEXT TO THE WORD PRETZELS (or on top of the line next to whatever product was selected). (FIG. 6).

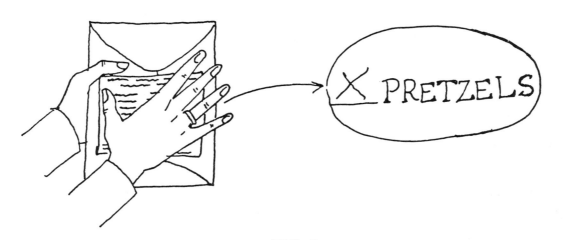

FIG. 6

It is at this moment, while you bring the envelope up to your nose to pretend to "smell" the pretzels, that your right third finger uses the "pencil ring" to make two quick intersecting lines, an X, next to the word pretzels. It is very important that it not appear that you're writing. Simply spot the location of the product that was selected as you are bringing the envelope up to your nose, use your left hand to steady the envelope, place your right hand palm down on the back of the envelope, and directly to the LEFT of the selection, pretend to smell (you can throw in a few sniffing noises for effect), and then make the X with your right third finger. (By the way, the reason you use cardboard to make the list is so that when you're making the X, you have a nice solid surface on which to write. If the list were typed on paper, as soon as you pushed down with the pencil lead, the whole envelope would buckle.)

Once you've made the mark, walk over to a member of the audience and hold the envelope up to his nose, asking him if he smells the pretzels. Whatever he says should get a laugh at this point. Smile and say, "Tell you what, rather then smelling my prediction, why don't you read it." Open up the envelope clasp, lift the flap, and remove the piece of cardboard and hand it to the audience member. AS YOU DO THIS, SAY, "WOULD YOU PLEASE READ OUT LOUD THE FOOD ITEM I PREDICTED MR. DRUCKER WOULD SELECT." If you deliver this line as a direct command, in a powerful voice, the audience member will look at the piece of paper, see the X next to the word pretzels, and say, "PRETZELS."

The fact that it says "I PREDICT MR. DRUCKER WILL SELECT:" across the top of the board, and there's an X next to the word PRETZELS, logically leads the audience member to assume that you have correctly predicted which product would be selected. And thus he reads the word PRETZELS out loud.

The key during your presentation is to act very confident, as if the word pretzels was in fact written ahead of time. Obviously some practice is required to get used to using the "ring pencil" without attracting suspicion. By the way, if you're concerned that somebody might detect the piece of lead attached to your ring, don't worry about it. First of all, it is concealed by your fingers and the back of your hand and, secondly, the audience isn't looking for a writing device, because you have convinced them that you wrote the prediction ahead of time. Right?!

TRICK #26

THE PREPCO FLOATING CROUTON ROUTINE

Sign in a South Carolina restaurant:
"Don't make fun of our coffee. You
may be old and weak yourself someday."

COMMENTS: For the purposes of helping to further stimulate your imagination and to illustrate that anything is possible, I've included this admittedly offbeat routine in the book. This trick was designed for the same PREPCO Christmas party I talked about in the previous trick. Since PREPCO is known in the food industry as the world's largest manufacturer of croutons, I wanted to include a trick in my show using croutons. However since croutons are difficult to see from the stage, I used big pieces of sponge to represent croutons. The following routine is the result.

DESCRIPTION OF TRICK: Holding up a 5" square sponge, the performer says to the audience (in this example consisting of PREPCO employees), "Ladies and gentleman, while this giant-size crouton may look fine, the fact is it's too moist." Holding the sponge over a bucket, the performer gives it a squeeze, whereupon water comes pouring out into the bucket. After dropping the soggy crouton into the bucket, the performer picks up a second crouton (sponge) and says, "This crouton looks okay too, but it's as hard as a rock." The performer taps a nearby table with the crouton, and the table breaks into pieces and falls to the floor! The performer just shrugs his shoulders and drops the second crouton into the bucket.

Finally, the performer says, "Of course neither of those two croutons measures up to the king of croutons, the Prepco crouton, which is not too moist and not too heavy; in fact you could say it is lighter than air!" As the performer says the following line, he turns on a tape recorder and then picks up a handkerchief. Suddenly, as the theme from "2001, A Space Odyssey" begins to play, a large 9" crouton, nearly twice the size of the other two, begins to rise from behind the handkerchief. Then it mysteriously floats back down behind the handkerchief. After this is repeated a couple of times, the performer suddenly throws the handkerchief into the air, and the giant "crouton" is gone, having vanished into the air!

THE SECRET: Believe it or not, a wire coat hanger is all that is needed to make the giant crouton float. The vanishing of the crouton is achieved by ditching the crouton into a box hidden behind your table, just before the handkerchief is thrown into the air.

MATERIALS: 3 large sponges like the kind used for washing cars, scissors, white glue, a ruler, a bucket, a shoe box and lid, 2 thumb tacks, two small tables, a piece of wood 15" x 15" x 1/2", a handful of nuts and bolts, a small tablecloth, a non-see-through handkerchief (a cloth napkin works great), a tape recorder with a tape of the theme from "2001, A Space Odyssey," wire cutters, pliers, and a wire coat hanger.

TO CONSTRUCT: Using the scissors and ruler, cut three pieces of sponge so that two of the pieces measure 5" square and one measures 9" square. If the sponges you bought aren't wide enough, glue layers of sponges together until your croutons are the correct dimensions.

Use the wire cutters to cut out a piece of wire in an L shape from the coat hanger. Next use the pliers to bend the top of the L into a series of little curls. These curls will enable you to "wear" the wire on the third finger of your right hand during the floating phase of the routine (FIG. 1).

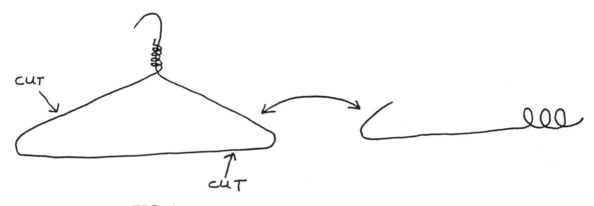

FIG. 1

Now coat the end of the L piece of wire with glue, and then jam the 9" crouton onto the end. Let dry. (FIG. 2).

FIG. 2

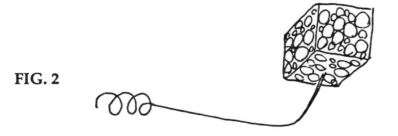

Next cut out two 1" x 9" strips from the lid of the shoebox and glue them to the back of the shoebox. Let dry. Now place the tablecloth over one of the tables and attach the two shoebox strips to the back of the table with the thumb tacks (FIG. 3)

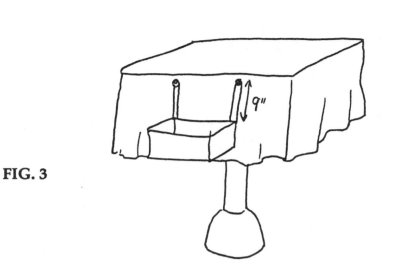

FIG. 3

What you have just made is known in magic as a "servante," and it is used for dropping objects into without the audience's knowledge.

Next take your second table and remove the top (usually there are four screws that you must unscrew). Place the 15" x 15" piece of wood on top of the exposed table base and place the handful of nuts and bolts onto the table top. You have just made your "break-a-part" table (FIG. 4).

FIG. 4

When you strike the table top with the crouton, the 15" piece of wood will fly up into the air, sending the nuts and bolts flying into every direction, creating the appearance that the crouton destroyed the table!

SET UP: Place the 9" crouton into the servante with the coiled end of the wire sticking up. Next place the tape recorder (with the tape cued) on top of the first

table. Now place the handkerchief on top of the table, over the tape recorder.
Next soak one of the 5" croutons in water for about 30 seconds, squeeze a little of
the water out, and set it, along with the other, dry, 5" crouton on the handkerchief.

Now set up your break-a-way table to the right of your performing table. Finally, set the bucket down to the left of the break-a-way table, and you're all set.

TO PERFORM: Pick up the water-filled crouton, hold it over the bucket and, as
you tell the audience how some croutons are too moist, squeeze the sponge.
After the audience laughs at this gag, drop the sponge into the bucket. Next
pick up the dry crouton and after talking about how some croutons are hard as
rocks, slam the crouton down onto the edge of the break-a-part table. This too
should get a laugh from the audience. Drop this second crouton into the bucket.

Now tell the audience how great PREPCO'S croutons are, and how they're
lighter than air, etc. Then reach under the handkerchief, turn on the tape recorder and then hold up the handkerchief, showing the front and the back to be
empty. Next bring the handkerchief down, over the table, and secretly slide
your RIGHT THIRD FINGER into the wire gimmick. Once you have the gimmick securely in place, bring the gimmick and the giant crouton up behind the
handkerchief (FIG. 5).

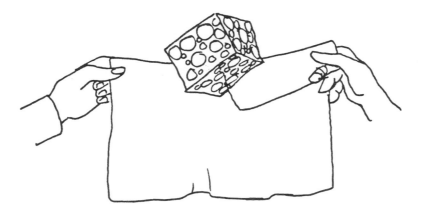

FIG. 5

As the music builds, use your third finger to slowly raise the crouton up into the
audience's view (BE SURE NOT TO LET THE AUDIENCE SEE THE WIRE!)
This will definitely receive a strong reaction. After making the crouton float up
and down behind the handkerchief a few times, slowly lower it back behind the

table and straight into the shoe box. Now remove your finger from the gimmick. Slowly bring the handkerchief back up in front of you, AS IF THE CROUTON WERE STILL THERE. Finally, take a few steps, and then toss the handkerchief up into the air, letting it float to the ground. Smile at the audience and take your bows.

FINAL COMMENTS: While I, of course, understand that this FLOATING CROUTON ROUTINE is probably not going to be of much use to you as is, it certainly gives you a lot of FOOD FOR THOUGHT (pun intended.) As you have probably surmised, almost any object can be made to float using the wire method. Thus you can develop your own routine based around the ideas I've given you here.

TRICK #27

5 CARD PRODUCT PREDICTION

*Classified ad in an Oklahoma City
newspaper: "Used tombstone for sale.
Ideal for a family named Jones."*

COMMENTS: This is a fantastic trick because not only does it feature your company's product, but it also gets members of the audience involved in the trick.

DESCRIPTION OF TRICK: After selecting five volunteers from the audience to come to the front of the room, the performer hands each one a piece of white cardboard, approximately 1 foot square, to hold in front of their chests.

Next the performer asks a sixth member of the audience to point to two of the five volunteers. This is done, and the two people selected are asked to take a step forward. Of these two, the audience member is asked to point to one. The person selected is asked to turn his card around. When the card is turned around a picture of the company's product is seen. The performer asks the other four volunteers to turn their cards over; the audience is astounded to see that there is nothing on them. The audience member has freely selected the only card with the company's product on it!

THE SECRET: This trick is based on what might best be called "sleight-of-tongue." While no physical manipulation is going on, the performer is actually manipulating the audience with his words. Although it appears that the audience member has a free choice, the fact is that he is ALWAYS going to end up selecting the volunteer holding the product card. Why? Because you know which person is holding the product card at the beginning of the trick. And thus no matter who the audience member chooses, you're going to INTERPRET his selection in such a way as to ELIMINATE those people holding blank cards, until you are eventually left with the one person holding the product card.

For example, if the audience member pointed to two volunteers, neither of whom was holding the product card, then you would have them take a step backwards, thus eliminating them from the demonstration. If on the other hand, one of the two people pointed to is in fact holding the product card, you would have them take a step forward, THUS ELIMINATING EVERYONE ELSE FROM THE GAME! Get the idea?

That's why it's important that you use the words "POINT TO," as opposed to PICK, CHOOSE OR SELECT. Saying "point to two people" is a way of getting the audience member to make a selection without you telling the audience what it is you are going to do with the selection. On the other hand, if you were to say, "CHOOSE TWO of the volunteers," then it's implied that you are going to do something with the two chosen individuals. And if neither of them happened to be holding the product card, you'd be up a river.

The key is to act as if you really couldn't care less which people are selected, as if the audience volunteer is really doing all the work and all you're doing is carrying out instructions. The fact is, nothing could be further from the truth. You are constantly using what they are saying to get the person holding the product card to be selected.

Now let's try a complete example. Let's say the volunteers are lined up 1 2 3 4 5, and volunteer #4 is holding the card with the product on it. Suppose the audience member points to volunteers 3 & 4. Then you would have those two step forward. Of those two, you would then ask the audience member to point to one of them. If he pointed to volunteer #4, then that's the one you would go with. If on the other hand he pointed to #3, then you would say, "Fine, would you please take a step BACKWARDS and join the other three people behind you. Thank you." And then you would focus all the attention on volunteer number #4, as if that's how you intended the selection process to take place all along!

Once again, it is crucial that you act as if everything that is happening is fair, and that you couldn't care less which people are selected. Any hesitation or slipup in your delivery will give you away. Another important key is to keep things moving quickly. Don't give the audience time to think too long. As soon as one set of selections is made, move the volunteers into position and get on to the next set of selections. The entire selection process should take less than 30 seconds.

Let's take another example. Suppose the audience member points to two people, neither of whom is holding the product card. What do you do? No problem; you very matter-of- factly say, "Great, would you two please take a step backwards... Now John, (the name of the selector), there are three people remaining, would you please point to two of them." Please note, YOU DID NOT INDICATE WHAT YOU WERE GOING TO DO WITH THE TWO PEOPLE HE POINTED TO. NO COMMITMENT WAS MADE ON YOUR PART.

If one of the volunteers he points to is holding the product card, you would say, "Super, and of those two, please point to one." If he points to the person with the product card, you say, "Are you sure that's the one you want? Remember it's up to you... It makes no difference to me... you have a free choice." The fact is, you want him to feel as if he really did have a free choice as to whom he finally picked. (At this point you may be thinking, "Isn't it a little dangerous to give him a chance to change his mind?" No it's not. The person rarely, if ever, changes his mind once he's arrived at a decision. After all, why should he; he had a free choice. Right!?)

If, on the other hand, he had pointed to the person not holding the product card, you would simply say, "Fine, and would you, sir, please take a step back... that leaves us with Pam" (the name of the person holding the product card). One way or the other, you're going to get the person holding the product card to be the last person standing in front.

Rather than going through all the possible combinations of what could happen, the best thing for you to do is to practice the trick a number of times. Have a friend point to two of five pieces of paper, one of which has an X drawn on the back of it. After a while you'll get good at moving him along to the paper with the X on it (which by the way, is not a bad trick in itself!)

I know I'm being redundant, but I want you to be absolutely clear on the fact that the strength of this trick depends on the audience not knowing exactly what it is you are doing. YOU DON'T EVEN MENTION THAT THERE IS ANYTHING ON THE BACK OF THE PIECES OF CARDBOARD UNTIL THE VERY END! Only when the last person is standing there holding the card do you reveal why you had each person come up to help. You say, "Now that John has freely selected one person who is holding a card, I'm going to let you in on a little secret. Before coming here today I placed a picture of one of your company's fine products on the back of one of these pieces of cardboard. Would everyone in the back row please turn their card around. (They do, and there is nothing on them.) "Now Pam, would you please turn your card around." She does and, miracle of miracles, there's the company's product!

TO CONSTRUCT: Get five pieces of white cardboard approximately 10 x 12 inches, and glue a picture of one of your company's products on the back of one of the pieces.

SET UP: Stack the five pieces of cardboard so that the one with the product on it is second from the top, product side down.

TO PERFORM: This is one of the those tricks where it's best not to say too much before performing it. Simply have five people come up on stage with you and hand each person one piece of cardboard, requesting that they hold the cardboard flat against their chest. Make sure you remember which person is holding the product card. If you always pass out the cards from left to right, the second person in line will always be holding the product card.

Now simply follow the presentation outlined above under THE SECRET.

At the conclusion of the trick, be sure to thank all of your participants for helping and send them back to their seats with a round of applause.

TRICK #28

"IT'S IN THE BAG" PRODUCT PREDICTION

*"If there's ever a question of your success,
look to your work and there's the answer."*

COMMENTS: The following trick, like the previous one, is a magical way to introduce a particular product to your audience. Although this version is completely different in both presentation and secret than the 5 CARD PRODUCT PREDICTION, it is still just as entertaining.

TRICK DESCRIPTION: The performer, who is addressing a stationery supply company (no pun intended), holds up a sealed envelope which he states contains a prediction. After giving the envelope to a member of the audience to hold, the performer asks for a volunteer to assist him in an E.S.P. experiment. Having found a volunteer, he invites her to join him on stage. Next the performer holds up 10 small pieces of cardboard, each containing the name of a different product which the company sells. The products listed on the 10 cards are: 1) Typewriter ribbon, 2) pencils, 3) index cards, 4) stationery, 5) erasers, 6) birthday cards, 7) legal pads, 8) paper clips, 9) notebooks, and 10) staples.

The performer hands the ten cards to the volunteer, requesting that she give them a shuffle. When she has finished, the performer has her drop the shuffled cards into a paper bag, which he shakes up and down to further mix the cards.

Next he asks the volunteer to reach inside the bag, without looking, and remove one of the cards. The performer then asks her to read aloud the name of the product on the card she chose. She says, "Pencils."

The performer then asks the person in the audience who is holding the prediction to come up on stage and open the envelope. The audience is amazed to see that the contents of the envelope are a bundle of rubber-banded PENCILS!

THE SECRET: The question, of course, is how did the performer know that the volunteer would select the piece of cardboard with the word pencils on it? The answer is that she had no choice. This is because inside the bottom of the bag were 10 pieces of cardboard all with the word pencils written on them. The 10 cards that contain the 10 different product names are placed into a secret pocket in the side of the bag. (I know, pretty sneaky.)

MATERIALS: Twenty 2" X 3 1/2" pieces of thin white cardboard, a black felt-tip pen, 2 lunch bags, scissors, rubber cement, a business envelope, 10 pencils, and a rubber band.

TO CONSTRUCT: (Obviously you can use any products for this trick, but for consistency's sake, I'll stay with the stationery supplies.) The first step is to make the trick bag. To do this, take one of the paper bags and cut along the dotted line as shown in FIGURE 1.

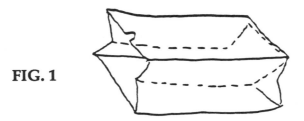

FIG. 1

Now carefully apply glue along the outside edges of this "half bag," and, while the glue is still wet, carefully slide it inside the unprepared bag (FIG. 2). Be sure to line up all three glued edges with the same matching parts of the normal bag. Let dry.

FIG. 2

You now have a gimmicked bag with a secret pocket in the side of it (FIG. 3).

FIG. 3

Next take the pen and carefully write the name of the 10 stationery products on 10 of the cards. Then write the word PENCILS on the remaining 10 cards and then drop them into the bottom of the bag (note: they DO NOT go into the secret pocket!)

Finally, place the rubber band around the pencils, place the bundle inside the envelope and seal it.

Place the "loaded" bag, the envelope, and the 10 product cards on your table, and you're all set to go.

TO PERFORM: After giving the prediction envelope to someone in the audience to hold, talk a few minutes about the company's many wonderful products. Then have a volunteer come up and shuffle the 10 product cards. Take the cards from her and place them into the bag, INSIDE THE SECRET POCKET. There should be no hesitation or fumbling at this point. If you hold the secret pocket open with your left thumb and first finger, it will make it easier for your right hand to drop the cards inside the pocket without any trouble.

Next give the bag a few shakes to "mix up the cards," and then let the volunteer reach inside and remove a card. Be sure to keep the secret compartment closed with your thumb and first finger so the only place she can take a card from is the bottom of the bag.

Once she has made her selection, set the bag aside, OUT OF VIEW OF THE AUDIENCE (if the bag is out of the sight of the audience, they are more likely to forget about it), and then have her read the name of the product on the card. Now have the prediction opened up on stage (so everyone can see the pencils), bringing this amazing feat of E.S.P. to its dramatic conclusion!

TRICK #29

THE JAMES RIVER TRADE SHOW ROUTINE

"No farmer ever plowed a field by turning it over in his mind."

COMMENTS: This routine was first brought to me by my good friend Mark Rosson, who runs a company called Magic Plus, which specializes in bringing magic to corporate events. Mark hired me to perform this routine for a company called James River, at their yearly trade show. James River is one of the country's largest distributors of toilet paper and other paper products.

I know that this routine is extremely commercial because at each one of my 12 performances throughout the day, a large crowd quickly gathered around the booth to watch the magic.

DESCRIPTION OF TRICK: With a crowd of paper products sales reps gathered around him, the performer holds up a new James River high-absorbency paper towel. He then says, "I have here the brand new "Dust buster II." This paper towel is so good at cleaning that it makes dust, dirt, grease and even LIT CIGARETTES DISAPPEAR. Suiting actions to words, the performer places a lit cigarette into the center of the towel. When he shakes out the towel, the cigarette has vanished!

Next the performer makes the towel into a cone as he says, "These towels are so well made they even absorb the nastiest liquid in the world, oil!" The performer proceeds to pour half a pitcher of oil into the cone. Upon unrolling the cone the oil is seen to have completely vanished! Continuing the performer says, "And the nice thing is, these towels are reusable, simply give them a squeeze and..." the performer squeezes the towel over a funnel and all the oil comes out of the funnel into a waiting tin can, "...they're as good as new!"

Opening up the towel the performer says, "I can tell that some of you out there watching this demonstration still aren't convinced that James River products are the best. Well let me prove it to you once and for all by showing you just how DURABLE our products are." The performer proceeds to tear the paper towel into pieces, then he takes out a magic wand and waves it over the torn pieces of paper. When he opens up the towel it is seen to be completely restored! The performer holds up the towel with a big smile on his face and says, "I hope you've enjoyed my magic, but if you really want to see some magic, step right up here and ask our James River sales reps how you can get a good deal on your next order of James River products!"

MORE COMMENTS: There you have it, a fast-paced audience tested 3 1/2 minute trade show routine. While you are probably not going to perform this exact routine, unless you happen to be hired by a paper-products company, I've included it in the book so you can see exactly how a professional trade show routine is put together. Feel free to adapt or change this routine any way you like. I hope that after reading through the tricks in this book, you have a pretty good idea how to customize a magic trick so that it fits your needs.

Since my main objective in putting this routine in the book is not to teach you new tricks, but to show you how to put together a trade show routine, I am not going to go into much detail on how the tricks are done. Those who are truly interested can go to any magic shop and purchase the necessary props.

THE SECRETS: Okay, here's a brief look at how each of the four tricks work. The first trick is the disappearance of a lit cigarette and it is achieved with the use of a thumb tip (see trick #13, THE VANISHING RED SCARF IN DOLLAR BILL, for a description of a thumb tip.) The second trick is the pouring of oil from a pitcher into the cone, and then the opening of the paper towel to show the oil has vanished. This is achieved by taking 3 cups of water and mixing it with orange food coloring to make the oil. The pitcher, which contains a gimmick which makes it look as if half the contents have been poured out, is sold under the name of "magic milk pitcher" and you can buy one in most magic shops. The third trick is the reappearance of the oil from the funnel (as the towel is squeezed over it), and this is achieved through the use of a gimmicked funnel which holds the "oil" inside it until you want it released, and it is also sold in most magic shops. Finally, the torn and restored paper towel is simply a modified version of trick #12, TURNING PROBLEMS INTO SOLUTIONS, only instead of crumpling up the napkin, you tear it up and then make the switch. Also, instead of using a watch you use a magic wand.

This routine is one of my favorites and I hope reading it has set the wheels of your mind into motion so that you are motivated to develop some of your own trade show routines!

TRICK #30

A Utility Production Box

"If you itch for success, keep on scratching."

COMMENTS: The UTILITY PRODUCTION BOX is basically a box that you can show empty, and then make appear in it any small size object(s) you desire. In the following example, we will pretend that our performer is a sales representative for the Kellogg's breakfast cereal company. As such, he will make boxes of cereal, along with some other goodies, appear from the empty production box.

DESCRIPTION OF TRICK: The performer starts off his presentation by directing the audience's attention to a bright blue box, without a top or a bottom, resting on a red wooden base. The front of the blue box has four 2" wide slits in it, enabling the audience to see into the box. What they see inside the box is a bright yellow cylinder. After lifting up the box and showing it to be empty, the performer replaces the box , and then removes the cylinder and shows it to be empty as well. At this point the audience can see through the slits in the front of the box that the box is indeed empty.

After replacing the cylinder in the box, the performer makes a few magical gestures, and then proceeds to reach into the cylinder and pull out eight boxes of single-serving-size breakfast cereal! These are followed by a spoon and a cereal bowl! The performer again shows the cylinder and box to be empty, claps his hands together, and then dramatically lifts off the box and the cylinder to reveal a giant pitcher of milk!

THE SECRET: The question, of course, is, "Where did all the objects come from?" The truth is, the objects were inside the cylinder throughout the entire trick. Then why didn't the audience see them? Because of a principle in magic called "Black Art."

Inside the yellow cylinder is another, slightly smaller cylinder covered with black velvet. Although the audience thinks they are seeing the inside of the blue box, which appears to be empty, what they are actually seeing is a second cylinder which is covered in black velvet. Because the inside of the box is also covered with black velvet, the cylinder blends in with the black background of the box and becomes invisible to the naked eye. (In the field of magic this is known as a "Black Art" effect.) Thus the cereal, spoon, bowl, and pitcher are inside the black cylinder the entire time.

While it will take you a bit more time to make this trick compared to some of the others in the book, the time spent will be well worth it. Once you've built it, you will have a versatile and dependable trick that will last for many years.

MATERIALS: Four pieces of 1/8" thick plywood 14" x 16", a 1/4 " piece of plywood 13" x 13", four little pieces of wood 1" x 1", two thick pieces of poster board — one black and one bright yellow, 2 yards of black velvet material, a can of 3M spray-on glue, scissors, two cans of spray paint — one bright blue and the other bright red, a bottle of white glue, a roll of 1" wide clear adhesive tape, a jigsaw, a box each of 1/2" and 1 1/2" finishing nails, and a hammer.

The dimensions I've given you will yield you a nice size production box. However, if you are speaking for a company whose product is larger then the given dimensions, simply change the plans as you see fit.

TO CONSTRUCT: Lay the four pieces of 14" x 16" wood on a piece of newspaper and spray paint them bright blue (FIG. 1). Be sure to get the edges. Let dry. (Note: It is only necessary to paint one side of the wood, as the other side will be covered with black velvet).

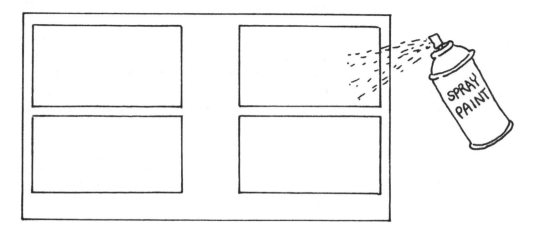

FIG. 1

Cut out four 14" x 16" pieces of black velvet. Now cover the four 14" x 16" pieces of wood with spray-on glue, and adhere a piece of black velvet onto the back of each piece of wood (the sides without paint on them), (FIG. 2). Let dry.

FIG. 2

Now take the jig saw and carefully cut out four 2" x 10" slats in the center of one of the pieces of wood (FIG. 3).

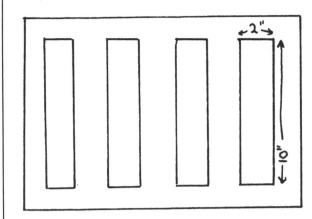

FIG. 3   FIG. 4

Run a line of glue around the edges of the four pieces of wood and assemble the four pieces together to form a box. Drive three 1/2" nails into the sides of the box for added reinforcement (FIG. 4).

Next you will construct the two cylinders. I will refer to the outer yellow cylinder the audience is aware of as the "outer cylinder." I will refer to the secret cylinder which the audience is never aware of, (and which will contain whatever it is you want to make appear) as the "inner cylinder."

To make the outer cylinder, cut off a piece of yellow poster board and form it into a cylinder measuring 15" tall by 13 " in diameter. Run a couple of pieces of clear adhesive tape along the seam to keep the cylinder intact (FIG. 5).

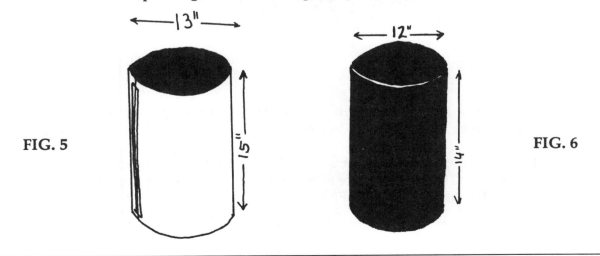

FIG. 5   FIG. 6

To form the inner cylinder, cut off a piece of black poster board and form it into a cylinder measuring 14" tall by 12" in diameter.   Run a couple of pieces of clear adhesive tape along the seam to keep the cylinder intact. Next cover the outside of the inner cylinder with black velvet (FIG. 6).

The last piece of equipment you need to construct is the base. To do this take the four 1" x 1" pieces of wood, and glue and nail them (using the 1 1/2" nails) to the four corners of the remaining 15" x 15" piece of wood (FIG. 7).

FIG. 7

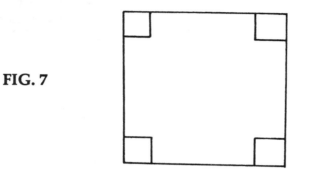

Next place the base on a piece of newspaper with the four "legs" of the base sticking up, and spray paint the bottom of the base bright red. When the paint has dried, flip the base over and line the top of the base with black velvet using the spray glue (FIG. 8).

FIG. 8

Great, you now have all four parts of the PRODUCTION BOX completed: The Blue box, the Yellow outer cylinder, the black velvet inner cylinder and the red base.
SET UP: To prepare the trick for performance, place the "inner cylinder" onto the center of the base. Next place everything you wish to make appear from the box inside the "inner cylinder" (FIG. 9).

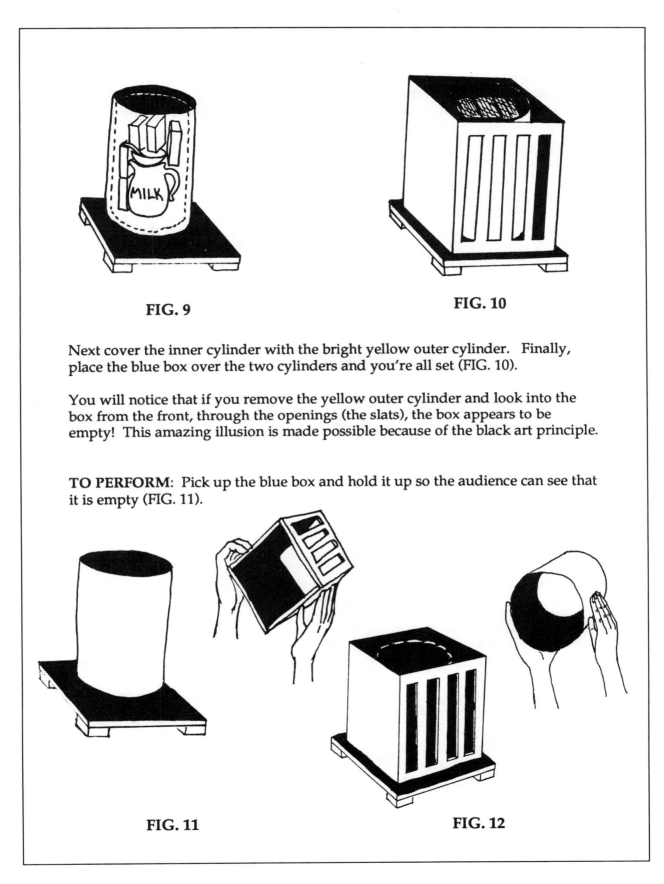

FIG. 9

FIG. 10

Next cover the inner cylinder with the bright yellow outer cylinder.   Finally, place the blue box over the two cylinders and you're all set (FIG. 10).

You will notice that if you remove the yellow outer cylinder and look into the box from the front, through the openings (the slats), the box appears to be empty! This amazing illusion is made possible because of the black art principle.

TO PERFORM: Pick up the blue box and hold it up so the audience can see that it is empty (FIG. 11).

FIG. 11

FIG. 12

Replace the box back on the base, making sure the slats are still facing the audience. Next, lift up the yellow outer cylinder from the box and show it to be empty (be sure not to disturb the inner cylinder when doing this). The audience can apparently see the box to be empty through the slats while you are showing the "outer cylinder" (FIG. 12). Replace the outer cylinder back inside the box, over the inner cylinder.

Now clap your hands over the box, make a magic gesture with them, and pull out the cereal boxes, followed by the spoon and bowl (FIG. 13).

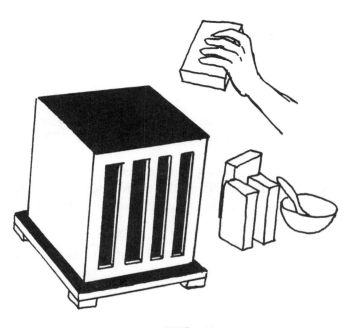

FIG. 13

After all these items have magically appeared, repeat the previous two steps of showing the box, and then the "outer cylinder" to be empty once again. After the audience is thoroughly convinced that there is absolutely nothing hidden in the box or the cylinder, lift off the box and set it aside. This will leave you with just the yellow cylinder on the base (with the secret cylinder and the milk pitcher still hidden inside).

For the finale, grasp the top edges of BOTH cylinders and lift them together as one unit, off the milk pitcher (FIG. 14). The audience will be amazed to see the appearance of a full pitcher of milk!

FIG. 14

This is the final trick in the book and, like all the rest of the tricks, it can be used to entertain, delight, amaze and inform. Enjoy!

PART VII

TEN DO'S AND DON'TS

1. Don't ever expose the secret to a trick when people ask. They'll just be disappointed.

2. Do Rehearse your tricks over and over in front of a mirror. There's no such thing as too much practice!

3. Don't be afraid to sit down and write out your OWN routines for the tricks in this book.

4. Don't try to learn every trick in the book. Start by picking out five or six that you really like and concentrate on perfecting those.

5. Do the tricks as often as possible — that's the only way you'll become good.

6. Do get feedback from your family and friends. They can often spot flaws that you can't see.

7. Don't rush through a trick. If you're enjoying the trick the audience will too!

8. Do see how many tricks in the book tie in with your product or service. That way, when a situation arises where you can incorporate a magic trick into your speech or presentation, you'll be prepared.

9. Don't worry about messing up a trick. If it happens, it happens. Learn from it and go on.

10. Do have a blast!!!

CONCLUDING THOUGHTS

Magic has been around for centuries because people enjoy being fooled. Not made fun of, but fooled. Please take care to treat your audience with respect, and you'll find they'll do the same for you.

I hope you've gotten as much joy out of reading this book and going through the tricks as I've had writing it. Magic is a fascinating field. It knows no boundaries — it appeals to people of all ages, from all segments of life, at every income level. Wherever you go in the world, magic can be a key to opening up doors marked opportunity, enjoyment, and friendship.

A BIZARRE STORY

Lastly, I'd like to leave you with this true story. I know it's true because it happened to me. However, before I tell it, let me say that while what we magicians do may look like real magic, you (after having read this book), and I know that everything a magician does is based on sound principles of science and theater. Real magic doesn't exist, right? Well maybe... Call it coincidence, call it luck, but the only thing I know for sure is that I have no explanation for the following story.

It happened one evening while I was performing at the Century Plaza Hotel in Beverly Hills. I had been hired to perform 2 hours of close-up magic for the annual Hunt Ball. This is a very prestigious affair with over 500 people in attendance. Everyone is dressed very elegantly, with the men sporting tuxedos and the women looking glamorous in their expensive evening gowns.

I arrived at the beginning of the cocktail hour and checked in with the host. Next, I walked over to a secluded corner of the ballroom to remove my tricks from my close-up case and place them into my various tuxedo pockets. As I was "loading up," I happened to glance down to the floor, where a shiny object caught my eye. I bent down and picked it up, whereupon I discovered it was an earring. It was a round black button type earring with a diamond in the center. I noticed it had a clip on the back.

My first impulse was to go find the host and turn it in to him, but then I thought, no, I'll just hang on to it for a while. I knew I could always turn it in at the end of the night if I didn't find a use for it. Shoving the earring into my left pocket, I quickly finished setting up.

Having hidden my case in a safe spot, I set about finding a group of people with whom to kick off my night. I generally take a moment or two and survey the room before I start performing. I like to pick out just the right group for whom to perform. After all, there's nothing worse than going up to your first group of the night and having them tell you they don't want to see any magic.

After scanning the room of more than 500 people, I spotted four women and a man standing together in approximately the center of the room, enjoying their drinks. They looked like a fun group, so I approached them. After introducing myself, I turned to the woman in the center of the group, (who I noticed had both her earrings on), and said, "Excuse me, Miss, there's something behind your ear." Whereupon I proceeded to pull out a silver half-dollar from behind her ear.

The lady who was standing next to her saw a glint of silver from the coin and said, "Oh, did he get your earring?" Then she said, "Oh, it's a coin." Well, after hearing this, I stuck my hand into my left pocket and I palmed out the earring. I thought I'd switch it for the coin and, since the lady had mentioned an earring, it would be a pretty neat trick. Well, I switched the earring for the coin, and when I opened up my hand and showed everyone the earring, the lady from whose ear I had pulled the coin let out a loud scream, and grabbed the "earring" from my hand. Next she proceeded to pull up her dress, whereupon I, along with everyone else, saw that on one of her shoes was a round black thing with a diamond in the center, clipped to the front of the shoe. The other shoe was missing its diamond clip-on ornament! Well, cut my legs off and call me shorty, of the more then 500 people in the room, I found the lady who the "earring" (shoe clip) belonged to! Kreskin, eat your heart out!

The lady who was standing next to her started saying, "Did he touch your foot, did you feel anything... how'd he get that?" And she said, "No, he never came near me, I swear!"

I just looked at the group, smiled, and said, "Not bad, huh!?" And then I spun around on my heels and walked away. Of course they weren't one tenth as amazed as I was!

I mean when you think about all the things that had to happen for this to take place... She had to lose the shoe clip in THAT corner of the room, then I had to come along and find it, then I had to hang on to it and not turn it in right away, then I had to pick them to go up to out of a room full of over 500 people, then I had to pull a coin out of HER ear, then the lady standing next to her had to say, OUT LOUD, "Oh did he get your earring?", then I had to make the decision to switch the coin for the "earring!"... Give me a break! What are the odds? It's magic. That's all there is to it. That's the only explanation there is. So now I can honestly say I BELIEVE IN MAGIC! How about you... Do you believe in magic?

RECOMMENDED READING

Other good books on magic that I highly recommend include:

MAGIC AND SHOWMANSHIP by Henning Nelms
(Dover Pub., New York, 1969)

THE MAGIC BOOK by Harry Lorayne
(G.P. Putnam's Sons, New York, 1977)

NOW YOU SEE IT, NOW YOU DON'T by Bill Tarr
(Vintage Books, New York, 1976)

PAUL DANIELS AND THE STORY OF MAGIC by John Fisher
(Jonathan Cape Ltd., London, 1987)

IMPROMPTU MAGIC FROM THE MAGIC CASTLE by Leo Behnke
(J.P. Tarcher, Inc., Los Angeles, 1980)

PARTY MAGIC FROM THE MAGIC CASTLE by Leo Behnke
(J.P. Tarcher, Inc., Los Angeles, 1980)

THE WORLD'S GREATEST MAGIC by Hyla M. Clark
(Tree Communications, Inc. New York, 1976)

THE COMPLETE ILLUSTRATED BOOK OF CLOSE UP MAGIC
by Walter B. Gibson
(Doubleday & Co. Inc., New York, 1980)

THE ILLUSTRATED HISTORY OF MAGIC by Milbourne Christopher
(Thomas Y. Crowell Co., New York, 1973)

THE COMEDY MAGIC TEXTBOOK by David Roper
(Snowflake Pub., Georgia, 1986)

MAGIC DIGEST by George B. Anderson
(DBI Books, Inc., Illinois, 1972)

ENCYCLOPEDIA OF IMPROMPTU MAGIC by Martin Gardner
(Magic Inc., Chicago, 1978)

THE GREAT BOOK OF MAGIC by Wendy Rydell & George Gilbert
(Harry N. Abrams, Inc., New York, 1976)

Michael Jeffreys is available for after dinner speeches, seminars, workshops, trade shows, and radio and T.V. interviews. You may contact him in Los Angeles at (213) 473-6291.

MY FAVORITE TRICKS

1.

2.

3.

4.

5.

6.

7.

8.

9.

10.

OTHER WAYS I CAN USE MAGIC TO
HELP PROMOTE MYSELF

1.

2.

3.

4.

5.

6.

7.

8.

9.

10.

THOUGHTS AND IDEAS